PASSION OF YOUTH

ALSO BY WILHELM REICH

WILHELM REICH

Passion of Youth

AN AUTOBIOGRAPHY, 1897–1922

EDITED BY MARY BOYD HIGGINS
AND CHESTER M. RAPHAEL, M.D.

With translations by Philip Schmitz
and Jerri Tompkins

PARAGON HOUSE
NEW YORK

First paperback edition, 1990

Published in the United States by

Paragon House
90 Fifth Avenue
New York, NY 10011

Published by arrangement with Farrar, Straus & Giroux, Inc.

Library of Congress Cataloging-in-Publication Data
Reich, Wilhelm, 1897–1957.
[Leidenschaft der Jugend.   English]
Passion of youth : an autobiography, 1897–1922 / Wilhelm Reich ;
edited by Mary Boyd Higgins and Chester M. Raphael ; with
translations by Philip Schmitz and Jerri Tompkins.—
1st paperback ed.
p.   cm.
Translation of: Leidenschaft der Jugend.
Reprint. Originally published: New York : Farrar, Straus, Giroux,
1988.
ISBN 1–55778–275–X
1. Reich, Wilhelm, 1897–1957—Childhood and youth.
2. Psychoanalysts—Austria—Biography.   I. Higgins, Mary (Mary
Boyd)   II. Raphael, Chester M.   III. Title.
BF109.R38A3   1990
150.19′5′092—dc20
[B]   89–22864
CIP

Manufactured in the United States of America

Love, work and knowledge are the wellsprings of our life. They should also govern it.

WILHELM REICH

Contents

Preface

We rarely catch a glimpse into the process by which great men develop, or experience intimately their passion, and their pain. Only the finished product—the mature person, the objective work—is presentable. Feelings of sexual need and desire, of love and hate, of longing, despair, frustration, and confusion lie buried in secrecy. Man's penchant for gossip and malicious intrusion may well express his need, however distorted, to break through this wall of secrecy and to learn the truth about his world and the great men and women whose lives "thrust it forward."

Wilhelm Reich was well aware of the danger implicit in this truth "in a world that was not ready to listen." But he was firmly convinced that it was essential to preserve it. In 1919, as a twenty-two-year-old medical student, Reich began to keep diaries and, during that same year, he wrote a recollection of his childhood and youth. Later, in 1937, he recalled his experiences in the Great War and his medical studies at the University of Vienna. These writings are now made available in order to dispel the myths given currency by the various biographies that have appeared since his death and to keep faith with the basic mandate of his will: "to safeguard the truth about my life and work."

In publishing this material, I have not lost sight of the essential: what Reich did, what he discovered, the tool of scientific knowledge he has placed in our hands. But, as a Nobel laureate remarked recently, "Science is made by people."

Mary Boyd Higgins, Trustee
The Wilhelm Reich Infant Trust Fund
New York, 1988

We tell ourselves that anyone who has succeeded in educating himself to truth about himself is permanently defended against the danger of immorality, even though his standard of morality may differ in some respect from that which is customary in society.

—SIGMUND FREUD,
Introductory Lectures on Psychoanalysis

ONE

Childhood and Puberty
1897–1914

My Childhood

I was born in a small village as the first child of not unprosperous parents. My father was a farmer who, together with an uncle of my mother's, had leased a fairly large landed estate in northern Bukovina, the farthest outpost of German culture. From the beginning, my mother tongue was German, as was my schooling. My parents considered it very important that I not speak the Yiddish of the surrounding population; they regarded it as "crude." The use of any Yiddish expression would bring severe punishment. The line separating my parents from the Orthodox Jews had a very material basis. In the agricultural business which my father ran, there were three types of workers: the daily workers, who were farmers from the surrounding villages; the farmhands, who were the paid employees in the business; and, lastly, the office workers, a number of whom were Jews—the manager, the steward, the cashier, and so forth. My father was not only a so-called free spirit but, as the boss, he had to keep himself apart from the Ukrainian population as well as from the Jewish administrative staff. The structure of the business was absolutely hierarchical and patriarchal.

The Hebrew language, unlike Yiddish, was an expression of reverence for the old Jewish tradition, built on a history of some six thousand years. Thus, there existed a Jewish aristocracy and great importance was attached to one's lineage. My father's father was famous as a "very wise man." He, too, had been a free spirit, a "thinker," who was held in timid regard by the Orthodox Jews but was highly esteemed by the Ukrainian farmers. He ran an agricultural establishment, but actually left business matters to his wife. He himself read many books, scolded the farmers, and counseled the women as best he could. He was, as they said, "cosmopolitan" and a "kindly friend" to the people. He adhered to the Jewish law, but only to avoid talk. Once, when I was about six, we visited him on the Day of Atonement, when Orthodox Jews fast. I was asked to call him from the prayerhouse to a meal. But they forgot to tell me to speak softly. I spoke loudly and in front of everyone. There was a great fuss and my father spanked me.

My father had invested all his liquid assets and received the major portion of his outside financial support from my great-uncle, who was already a wealthy man. Father was a modern person, and even though he was never reckless with money but was rather shrewdly frugal, he had to work very hard so as not to fall behind financially while still keeping up a comfortable home.

A second child arrived a year after me; it was a girl, but she died soon after birth. Two years later, my brother, Robert, was born and, as his birth was also a difficult one, it became necessary for my mother to be away at a spa on two or three occasions.

It is from this date that my recollections begin to grow clear. There is one scene which I can still envision vividly in all its detail: My brother must have been a year old, and I four. Mother was away and had left us in the care of the servants, a fact which was to play an important part in my later development, especially in regard to sexuality. We had three servants: a cook; a housemaid, who was a country girl; and a nurse for Robert. Father had gone to the city for the day on business and was not expected home until about ten o'clock. My brother and I were playing in the kitchen on the bed of one of the servants. Suddenly my brother let out a scream. I was terrified, for I had a great fear of the beatings which were so amply meted out by my austere father. And at that moment Father did, in fact, come in and ask what had happened. Naturally, I could not answer; the nurse told all. As our "family doctor" (who was also the steward of our estate and had great practical experience in such matters) later stated, I had dislocated my brother's tiny arm. I can still see him lying there on the bed, dressed only in a baby shirt and screaming at the top of his voice.

Our steward reset the arm while I cowered in a corner, waiting for what was to come. However, to my great astonishment, it did not happen. My father only looked at me with that terrible expression which, even when I was older, made me tremble and which always heralded trouble.

I cannot remember my father ever having cuddled or treated me tenderly at that time—nor can I recollect feeling any attachment to him (I should like to emphasize *at that time*).

A second experience which either immediately preceded or followed the above and to which I attach great significance will serve to illustrate the first phases of my *conscious* sexuality.

As I have already mentioned, we children lived with the servants. Father was always away on trips, since he loved Mother very dearly and could not stand being at home when she was not there. Robert and I slept with his nurse, all in the same bed. I recall that, even then, women were a mystery to me. As proof of this, I offer the fact that I do not remember (nor has anyone ever mentioned) that I asked adults the well-known children's questions such as "Where do babies come from?" etc. I do know very well, however, that I had been brooding over this and similar problems long before this period and had never asked those questions because I sensed something *verboten*.

Our housemaid was having an affair with the coachman, a young, good-looking farm boy who had work to do in the house every evening and often staged humorous little skits in the kitchen when Father was away.

One evening when he was with us, I was on the lookout for his every glance or gesture. I watched him reach down in the vicinity of his genitals. He cast a laughing glance toward his girl, raised his fingers to his mouth, licked them, and clicked with his tongue, which was probably meant to imply, "It tastes good." He noticed my curiosity and with a laugh instructed me how to perform this gesture. I enjoyed doing this very much and repeated it several times "charmingly" to the amusement of all present.

Another time he visited his girl and I eavesdropped on their sexual act. This produced in me erotic sensations of enormous intensity. (I was approximately four and a half years old.)

On a subsequent afternoon, the nurse was lying in bed with Robi. I crawled in and joined them because, so I claimed, I wanted to take a nap. It is obvious, though, that I had other motives. The prostrate position of the girl with her exposed breasts had excited me and in effect I wanted to do what the coachman had done with the housemaid, namely, have intercourse. The nurse calmly allowed me to proceed; I climbed on top of her, lifted her dress, and reached feverishly for her genitals (to her apparent enjoyment). Her hair excited me particularly (I always slept with the maid, and several times before this I had made believe I was asleep and touched her genitals, plucking at the hair. After quite some time she would awake, hit me, and threaten to tell Father. Usually I stopped for a few days and then began anew). I should like to mention that I did not make any coital movements but that her vagina did twitch with my penis. I cannot say for sure whether I was erect, but presumably I was. This activity had gone on for a good ten minutes when my brother awoke, saw the caper, and called out, "I'm going to tell Papa," whereupon he got straight out of bed and toddled through the door in his little red shirt. Naturally, I was terrified once again, jumped down, and ran after him. But it was too late, for Father had just come from the farmhouse and had already been informed of the "good news" by the little fellow—although I do not know how. I did not receive a beating but was no longer allowed to sleep with the maid.

Among the other experiences I had during this period, and which I can only relate from my parents' accounts, were the following: I was with a large group (my parents, an uncle, and his family) in the public park in Czernowitz. My uncle took me up in his arms and I slapped his face, to the amusement of everyone present. I have always hated people with fat, oily faces. I don't know why. Mother and Father were slim and well built. But this uncle of my mother's, who later brought about my father's financial ruin, was a fat millionaire and large landowner. To me, he was an abomination.

On another occasion (I recall this only very vaguely) we were again in the park—I was two years old at the time. A little girl with a pretzel in her hand walked past us. I rushed at her, tore the pretzel away, gave her a push, and ran off. She began to cry, whereupon I went back to her, broke the pretzel in two, gave one half to her, and kept the other half for myself.

I link both incidents, especially the first, to my pronounced sadistic component and acquisitiveness and think I am not incorrect in tracing my present frantic, ruthless ambition back to this trait. However, other factors contributed heavily to the development of my ambition as well. But they, too, will be discussed later.

It is also said that when my brother was shown to me just after his birth I tried to strike him and called out, "I don't need a brother!" I would not be justified in connecting the incident to a mother complex by virtue of this one remark, for I cannot recall any other actions during that period which would have indicated the same. I must mention again that after my brother's birth my mother spent a long time at spas—I think it amounted to two years, with interruptions, and I therefore had no opportunity for close contact with her. I do remember clearly, though, that later I felt a much greater fondness for her than for my father. Today, nine years after her death and five years after Father's, my yearning for maternal love (which possibly manifests itself in my substituting the love of women who are like her) is greater than that for paternal affection, despite the fact that my relationship to my father improved significantly after Mother's death, and despite the fact that I view his death as the most crucial event in my life thus far.

I should now like to continue with a description of the period following ages three to five.

Mother soon recovered her health and returned home. I shall always treasure among my happiest memories the family life that started then.

At age six, I began to learn the primary-school subjects. Mother and Father took turns teaching me reading, writing, and arithmetic, and it was at that point that I felt the full extent of my father's strictness. For the slightest mistake or lapse of attention he struck me, made me eat in the kitchen or stand in a corner. This is the period during which he laid the foundation for my ambitiousness, a characteristic which today I often find distasteful, yes, even revolting. My mother always protected me from his blows by standing between us, and I finally begged that only she give me instruction. She promised, on the condition that I really apply myself. And that I did! Under her guidance, I made excellent progress. How vivid the picture is before me: Mother sitting at the table, with her kind eyes, delicate profile, and the distinctive set of her mouth. In her never-idle hands she holds her knitting, before her is my exercise book and I next to it, writing as she dictates. How often her hand stroked my long hair, how concerned was her cry of "Start writing!" whenever she heard Father coming from a consultation with officials or the workers!

I do not wish to be sentimental, but I involuntarily choke up at these memories. How I long for the blissful happiness of childhood, and how little the help or protection of a father means to me! I wish he, too, were alive, but not as a supporting guardian, because it is now, since his death, that I have matured to full adulthood. Only as a person in his own right would I have him back, for when Mother died, we found each other and became true friends—rather than just father and son.

Today my yearning for Mother is greater, due to the fact that I no longer need a man to protect me yet I do need a woman's love—but wait! I cannot doubt the attachment to my mother, for not only my yearning for the tender touch of a woman's hand is traceable to her but, as just occurred to me, the girls to whom I have felt attracted have always been peaceful, gentle types, and all of them with a soft expression around the mouth. However, I do have a preference for blondes, while my mother's hair was dark.

The roots of my initially poor relationship to my father lay very deep; they were closely connected with my having black hair and eyes, traits inherited from my maternal grandmother, with whom Father had a typical mother-in-law relationship. I was always Mother's favorite, while my brother—a golden blond—was Father's.

Still another fact is significant: during this period (ages five to ten) I remember next to nothing about my brother. This can probably be explained by the fact that my attachment to Mother and the mutuality of this feeling gave me no cause to fear competition from him. (Later I found living with him extremely difficult.) On the other hand, my indifference (if not something stronger!) toward Father was rooted partially in his attitude toward me and partially in my fear of him as a rival. In addition, I sided with Mother for the following reason (which subsequently provoked the family catastrophe): despite Mother's fervent love, and even adoration of Father, he grew extremely jealous of her, and this was outright torture for her. Father was quite her opposite, in that he had a ferocious temper, although he was an extremely kind, intelligent, and knowing person. Mother trembled with fear (literally!), as did I, when he was "excited," no matter if the reason for this lay within the household or elsewhere. My brother also has a bad temper, and since he resembled Father and Father's family in other respects, he was constantly held up as a "true" man, compared to me, who never had a temper but was always inclined to hold a grudge. Father also placed much greater demands on me than on Robert as far as work was concerned. I recall the following incident which took place when I was seven years old: We had a governess who was preparing me for the entrance examinations for the regular school. One day I was writing as she dictated in the children's room, the window of which opened onto a garden. Father came to the window and had a look at the notebook. I was trembling in anticipation and stood there with my head lowered for what I knew would surely come. And how correct I was! Father's austere voice rang out from the window: "Come here!" I obeyed and had my ears boxed for having made a slight mistake. As an additional punishment, I was also sent to eat in the kitchen.

As a child, I was strictly forbidden to play with the peasant and servant children. Until I was twelve, apart from my brother, I had no playmates. I often stood by our courtyard fence gazing longingly at the other children. Once I was playing by the fence and a peasant boy my age was watching me from a few meters away. Suddenly he grabbed a stone, I presume as a joke, and threw it at me. It hit my forehead and I bled a little. He certainly had not intended to be mean. My mother washed my forehead and told my father what had happened. Father became enraged. He summoned the child and the child's father. After referring briefly to the incident, he gave the father a dreadful beating. The peasant endured it quietly, without defending himself. As he walked off with his child, I could see him beating him the whole way home. The boy screamed frightfully. I was very upset, but said nothing and crept away to hide. I was about eight years old. I both hated and feared my father. But the submissive attitude of the peasant must have left a deep impression on me, an impression of my father's power. His power over the servants and peasants was in fact enormous. Whoever spoke to him had to take off his hat. If anyone forgot, his hat was sure to fly off with a blow.

One scene remains unforgettable. Every Saturday, all the many workers were paid. They stood in a row, and my father walked along the row with the manager and the cashier and paid them. This time, a coachman came by with supplies he had purchased in town. He was a little drunk and reeled slightly as he approached my father to give him a message. When my father noticed his condition, he cuffed him so hard that the man fell to the ground. I stood there filled with fear, fear of two kinds:

What will the peasants do now? and: How dreadful my father can be! Nothing happened! The paying went on calmly.

It was only after my father's death that I examined his personality for its good as well as its bad character traits. I should like to mention only two of my current findings: He was a person whose narcissism was quite strongly pronounced (although this pertained more to the intellectual than to the physical realm), as was his sadism, for we know that all individuals with quick tempers are more or less sadistic.

He was very proud of himself and his family and favored my brother because of his physical and intellectual qualities.

I am thoroughly convinced that his love for my mother was genuine and deep, for he was a forthright, openhearted person. Proof of this may be seen in his tragic fate four years after her death.

But Mother suffered dreadfully from his jealousy and sudden temper, although she bore it with quiet submission and without resistance. I shall have to go into this issue in detail later on.

Family life at our house during this period (ages five to ten) was truly ideal, with the exception of incidents which must certainly occur in all families.

Father prospered financially, although never brilliantly, because of his honesty. He put nothing aside but lived within his means in accordance with his and his family's needs. We occupied a house with eight rooms, in addition to side rooms, and thanks to Mother's sense of orderliness, every corner of the house was pleasantly livable. Our education was channeled in the best possible directions, with the exception of a few errors stemming from the general trend in those days. For four years we had a highly intelligent girl living in our home to teach and educate us. There was also no lack of merry get-togethers, sometimes at home and occasionally in town. We lived as one can live only in the country, close to nature. Father was well known and esteemed in his own circles in town, and Mother's kindness and gentleness captured hearts wherever she went.

Father often joshed with our tutoress, S., who was a thoroughly decent girl, but this arose more from his excellent spirits and almost constant good humor than from any ulterior motives. He found it particularly amusing to make the girl blush, partly by way of delicately disguised erotic puns and partly through direct audacity (I must emphasize that I am entirely sure he had no ulterior motives)—but always in Mother's presence. Mother responded with complete indifference, sometimes she even enjoyed it in the way that married women often take a lively pleasure in the game of "virginal chastity." It is a well-known fact that women who are married themselves find enormous satisfaction in helping their unmarried friends to find similar happiness. However, I do not think that Father's easy manner made no impression at all on Mother! An isolated incident might have had no impact, but there may have been a cumulative effect which played an important role in the later catastrophe.

Our tutoress was also the object of my desire. Once I actually lay down on top of her while she was taking an afternoon nap, and fantasized having intercourse with her. Even now, I cannot understand why she allowed this. Was it "fun" for her, too, or was she not aware of what I had in mind? (Probably the former.) The following recollection gives rise to this assumption: One afternoon, Mother and she were sitting on the lawn in front of our house. I had just finished a drawing and came out of the children's room to show the tutoress what I had done. She praised me highly and said that as a reward I might stay with them for a quarter of an hour. I was overjoyed and quickly lay down next to Mother, with my head in her lap. Apparently they had just been interrupted in a conversation on some sexual matter, for when Mother began to speak again, she veiled the meaning of her words. Since there were no secrets for me, even at that age, I understood it all. They were discussing S.'s future husband. Suddenly Mother looked at me and said, with a laugh (I cannot remember exactly the words she used): "In seven years Willy will be grown up too, or do you think he might even be able to help you now?" (I was "grown up" in less time than that, in the sense that Mother had used the expression—and can still remember the feeling of pride I had, naturally without showing it, when I heard her say this.) I soon discovered the close connection of this remark to S. and their earlier conversation and several times a day during that period fantasized having intercourse with S.

In the late afternoon we very frequently drove to the river, about an hour away, to go swimming. Since I always bathed with Mother (S. did not), sexual feelings regularly stirred within me and I often attempted to undress Mother with my eyes.

One of our farmhands had a son approximately twenty years old who was a complete idiot. All day long, he would lie in the sun in front of the house, wearing only a shirt, and play with his genitals while mumbling unintelligible sounds. I enjoyed watching him play with himself and, through this, experienced highly pleasurable sensations. I cannot say whether or not my later intense pleasure in masturbating, which lasted for so many years, is rooted here. It is quite probable, however, due to the intensity of my sensations while watching the idiot and his performance. But this is not to say that I wouldn't have succumbed to masturbation apart from this incident.

I also enjoyed watching the men catching fish in the fish pond. They were either completely naked or wore only shirts. Here again, it was the pubic hair as well as the hair on their legs which attracted my attention. I might also have wondered why I myself had none.

According to my parents' later accounts, I was a well-behaved and diligent child in all other respects. I worked all day and always tried to complete my assignments to the satisfaction of the tutoress, yet my behavior was subdued and frequently even glum, which caused my father to call me "sourpuss."

How could I have been different after hearing the answers Mother or Father gave to Robi's questions about sex, or the talk of "the birds and the bees" which they employed when referring to such matters among other people when we children were present.

My brother was much moodier than I and very often dissolved

into tears, at the slightest cause. But he was always pampered and cuddled; he was also a much more beautiful child than I, with his long, curly blond hair and pretty blue eyes. And he was an enormous "little fatty," as my parents called him.

I had few opportunities to be away from home, with the exception of two trips to our grandmother in L., and to Uncle Bernhard, a brother of my father's who was a lawyer in S., as well as our trips to Czernowitz.

I recall the following incident which took place on one of the trips to our uncle's. I was playing "trains" on the parquet floor of the dining room with a female cousin who was twelve (i.e., five years older than I). As my uncle's wife was quite taken aback at this, Father forbade me to continue the game. I immediately hung my head and he ordered me, in a severe tone of voice, to leave the room.

On another occasion, when that same cousin and aunt were visiting us, she and I tore off the tail of my wooden hobbyhorse and stuck a silver spoon in. The spoon was found several years later, when we moved and the hobbyhorse was moldering in the attic.

In contrast to my mother, whose demands were very modest, my maternal grandmother (who lived with her husband in L.) took a great deal of pleasure in all the latest styles. In general, she looked very youthful, had not a single gray hair as yet, and was altogether more of a whorish than a motherly type, in Weininger's sense of the word. Thus, she also enjoyed dressing up Mother with clothes and jewelry. Nor, much to Father's annoyance, had she relinquished the maternal prerogative of exerting her influence in various ways. This fact has great importance in understanding the events that were to come.

The following incident will serve as an excellent illustration of the relationship between Father, Mother, and Grandmother. I was approximately six and a half or seven years old when Mother and I went to Grandmother's to visit. I enjoyed being at her house not only because of her kindness—she adored Mother and me—but also to no small extent because of the sense I had of having escaped Father's severity for a little while.

At that time, Mother bought herself a hat as well as several other things and then reported this most dutifully to Father, giving him all the prices. Today I no longer remember whether it was the independence exhibited by Mother in buying herself clothes without his approval, or whether it was the fact that she had been influenced by his mother-in-law, which moved my father to write a harsh letter saying, in so many words, that he was not willing to waste money on trash. Several days later, he appeared personally to take us home. When he arrived, Mother was cool toward him because of the letter, and I pressed close to her and did not greet him, despite his calling me over. He reproached me for this behavior for years to come and said it was characteristic of my personality. The fact that Mother was made to suffer for this incident for a long time is, unfortunately, a well-established fact.

Mother was a thoroughly good soul who loved both Father and Grandmother dearly but was caught between the devil and the deep blue sea if only because of the mother-in-law relationship. Grandmother sent me ten kronen each year for my birthday. It was after the above incident, around the time of my birthday, that an argument arose one evening between Father and Mother. Father was already lying in bed; Mother and I were still up. Suddenly Father shouted that I should give him the ten kronen I had received that very day from my grandmother. I obeyed, and Father set the money aflame with a candle. Mother made no remark but sat in the next room, quietly weeping.

My great-uncle, Grandmother's brother, had bought an estate near ours. Father, an academically trained agronomist, equipped it for him completely so that all he had to do was move into the manor and take over the administration. He knew very little about farming but had enough money, even at that time, to pay a hardworking, responsible steward. He had married for the second time—in fact, a woman twenty years younger than he, much to the annoyance of my father, for Robert and I were his sole heirs, in the absence of any other relatives. His aged mother, i.e., our great-grandmother, a spry woman of about eighty, moved in with him. She was enormously greedy, bossy, and mean, "the true mother of her even truer son," as my father put it.

Every summer, when Uncle went away with his wife, the old lady would come and stay with us for six or eight weeks. This never made Father very happy and, indeed, sharing the house with her was no joy. She involved herself in everybody's business. She was easily annoyed or would grow sullen, frequently at the slightest incidents; she refused to speak for days on end or made scenes—in short, she was a nuisance to everyone.

During this time my grandmother's husband died, and soon after, she moved in with us. It was our uncle's wish, too, that our great-grandmother should live with us, so that mother and daughter could be together. From that time on, the household was pure hell. Mother suffered most from this, for Father would simply not allow himself to be disturbed. In general, he always followed the dictum: "If there is something on your mind—out with it!" Luckily, this state of affairs lasted only one year. We then moved to a different estate and Father adamantly refused Uncle's demand that he take both Grandmother and Great-grandmother into his home.

The estate was located several kilometers from the imperial highway and connected with it by a bumpy country road which was extremely dangerous in bad weather. It led over three hills and four valleys, one of which was always swampy close to the road, and a source of the most outlandish stories and tales— for example, that ghosts walked the swamp by night, that one could even see phantom lights, for the body of a murdered man lay there whose "soul could not find the gateway to heaven." The region really was desolate, not a tree or bush far and wide; bleak, stripped soil, and the swamp. In the winter, wolves prowled there, and when one morning a worker reported that only the boots, some traces of blood, and torn bits of clothing of a farm woman had been found, our fear reached its height. Whenever we passed the swamp, we pressed close to our parents (especially at night), and along this piece of road the coachman had to keep a bundle of straw ready to light, because, it was said, wolves were afraid of fire. Father was actually attacked by wolves one winter and escaped a horrid death only through the coachman's presence of mind. Whenever Father went into town and was not expected home until late at night, Mother and I would linger at the window which faced in that direction, watching anxiously for the coach lights to appear.

Through constant contact with the servants we had grown very superstitious, to the extent that no cat or mouse could scurry through the room, no farm woman cross the road with empty buckets, no dog howl, without its being interpreted as an omen of something horrible. And when the interpretation of a commonplace event of this sort was confirmed (which can easily happen by chance once in a hundred times), our superstitions were reinforced. One evening the chambermaid came into the house filled with dread and reported that the dog on his chain was howling so terribly that we had better brace ourselves for an awful catastrophe. She added, however, that she did not know whether the dog was pointing its snout toward the heavens or toward the earth when it howled. In the first instance, it would mean a conflagration; in the second, death. One or two evenings later, an alarm was sounded throughout the entire village. We rushed outside and saw a column of fire reaching up to the sky from the direction of a barn which was full, since it was harvest time. The whole area was brightly illuminated for a radius of ten kilometers. Fortunately, the wind had turned away from the village, so that it was not in danger. Soon, however, the grain sheds in the fields within a distance of two kilometers caught fire and the whole horizon was a flaming inferno. Extinguishing the blaze with the fifty-liter village pump was out of the question, and thus, all that was done was to equip the farm boys with buckets and wet down the thatched roofs of our buildings.

The fire raged for ten days. The damage was inestimable, because the whole crop had been brought in. Fortunately, Father had insured his grain, as always, and suffered only a moderate loss.

The dog had apparently howled with its snout toward the heavens.

THE CATASTROPHE

I view the time just described, up to the age of ten, as the happiest period of my life.

The next phase, from age ten to approximately eighteen, not only influenced the direction of my later development but also contains a great many events which were of grave consequence for our family. It includes the catastrophe which destroyed, first, Mother, then Father, and finally my youth (and, partially, Robert's), as well as our beautiful domestic happiness. The deep inner causes for this I have already sketched in the previous section. Later, I shall return to them and give a brief summary. My intention now is to consider and describe the situation from a strictly subjective standpoint, neither as son nor as judge.

The groundwork for the disaster was laid the day my father asked me whether I wanted to attend the Gymnasium in town or study at home under the guidance of a tutor. How vividly I still see Father and Mother talking in their bedroom. I was in the children's room when Mother came in teary-eyed and took me to Father, who asked me which I preferred. I remained silent for a while, as I really was undecided; all that I had heard about attending a public school and about life in town drew me, while at the same time I was touched by Mother's tears, which were imploring me to remain with her. Finally, my wish to stay at home gained the upper hand—not because it seemed more desirable (after all, I had never known anything else) but simply because I wanted for once to do my parents a "favor." Oh, that I had never done so! Mother immediately showered me with kisses and promised me heaven on earth as a reward for sparing her the painful separation.

Father engaged a law student from the university to prepare

me for the entrance examination and to give me instruction later in all the Gymnasium's required subjects.

I still recall very clearly the feeling I had that evening when Father arrived with H. I was timid, either because I feared the transition from being educated under the guidance of a woman to being taught by a man, or due to the respect I felt at having a "real" university student before me. It turned out to be not so bad after all, for soon we were fast friends, although he permitted no nonsense while we were at work. I had to curve my fingers, hold them stiff, and receive a sharp rap on my fingertips—common educational practice in those days! He also had a way of spurring me on, not by force but through accomplishment based on independent motivation, on my own incentive rather than that of others. Soon he introduced me to the world of German literature, beginning with Karl May and gradually rising to Peter Rossegger and other popular poets, to Schiller and Kleist, and to the beautiful tales and stories of Hauff, which, among others, provided so many pleasurable hours.

But we were also given physical training—gymnastics and track as well as a variety of other sports—and on free afternoons, if I had been behaving well, walks into the surrounding countryside. He encouraged me to catch butterflies and in time I had put together a most beautiful collection of these colorful insects (which was later destroyed during the Russian invasion). He awakened in us country children a love of nature by taking us on all-day hikes into the forests and mountains. He would drive us on over stick and stone until we dropped exhausted in the shadow of a beech tree, dug into the "feed bag," and made short work of it. In that period my sexual desire seemed to diminish, for I can recall nothing of that sort during those years.

In the summer, I passed the entrance examination and was both proud and impatient for the time when I was to begin studying Latin—oh, the grandeur of the word alone!

The ardently desired moment soon arrived and I addressed myself with fiery zeal to studying Latin vocabulary. The winter passed without any major events, and after the first semester I brought home a report card with the top grade in every subject. Robert (who was still in primary school) did likewise, and thus everything progressed satisfactorily.

An incident which was a source of pain for Father, especially, occurred while we were taking a pleasure ride. Father, H., P. (one of Grandmother's young nieces), and we children were along. We were using a high, single-seat tilbury drawn by spirited young sorrels driven by Father himself. H., Robi, and I were sitting in the back, Father and P. in the front. He was busy with all kinds of flirtatious nonsense, and not paying close attention. All at once, we drove over a milestone and the high, light carriage tipped over to the right. Unfortunately, there was a deep ditch about a meter wide on that side of the road. I jumped off, as did H., who had taken six-year-old Robi by the arm. I saw P., who had been sitting on the left, hurled off the carriage in an arc. Father was lying in the ditch, trying to restrain the startled horses. H. helped him to his feet and asked if he was hurt, for he looked extremely pale. When he replied that he had a pain in his shoulder H., who was a strong person, began to "reset" the arm; i.e., began to pull on it with all his might. We then went home, and Father, Mother, and H. drove right into town to a surgeon whom they knew. Unfortunately, he was not in, so Father had to be treated by a different doctor, who put the arm in a cast, saying that it had been wrenched from its socket and, apparently, the ligaments were torn as well. He was to return in eight days. It is impossible to describe how Father suffered. Night after night he paced back and forth in his room, his teeth clenched in pain. After three days he went into town again, but this time he saw the surgeon with whom he was acquainted. After the cast was removed and the arm examined carefully, the surgeon remarked that, had the cast stayed on for the full eight days, Father would have had to say goodbye to his arm. Important ligaments had been torn and the articular capsule was distended, so that the articular head had been dislocated to the axilla. Then Father had to travel to a sulfur spa in Hungary, where he stayed for eight weeks. When he returned home, he was unable to raise his arm above a horizontal position, although this in itself spelled progress. With the help of special apparatus, which Father had acquired on the surgeon's advice and which was to strengthen the somewhat atrophied arm through activity and therapeutic exercises, he gradually regained complete use of his arm and hand.

Through my jump, I incurred a left inguinal hernia, which was soon followed by orchitis. When I returned from town with Mother after seeing the doctor, who prescribed a truss, I was met at the gate by P. In reply to her question about what the doctor had said, I proudly showed off the area of the hernia and allowed her to touch the truss. This elicited a rebuke from Mother which I could not understand. It is, however, noteworthy that both my brother and I were always very proud of ourselves for being ill and frequently exaggerated our ailments. This is readily understandable in view of the extra tenderness shown to us during periods of illness.

In the spring of 1907 we moved to another estate but had to live in a run-down building for several months because the house being built to Father's specifications was not yet finished. The house was situated close to the road and surrounded by a large area which was intended as a flower garden, although that plan was never realized. In back there was a large orchard as well as stables and barns and a fence separating them from the steward's farmhouse and the village.

As I mentioned above, we spent some time living in the house of a farmhand, where I tried to have intercourse with the maid again after a long interval, but I wasn't successful. My general condition at this age (ten and a half years old) was one of sexual hyperesthesia. Once I witnessed a mare being covered and was outright shocked at the size of the stallion's penis. After that, the sight of urinating stallions, cows, dogs, etc., produced pronounced sexual sensations in me. One of my favorite activities was to go into the stall at noon, while all the farmhands were eating or sleeping. I wantonly enjoyed observing the genitals of both male and female animals. While doing this, I always had an erection—something which had already been bothering me for some time. I had not yet masturbated and was equally innocent regarding nocturnal emissions.

One day I grew so excited looking at the animals that I took a whip with a smooth grip, turned it around, and thrust the handle into the vagina of a mare. The animal was surprised at first but then seemed to enjoy it. She spread her legs wide and began to urinate while I had an orgasm (without ejaculation). From then on, I did this every day and extended my activities to other mares as well, although I never could understand why their reactions were so varied. Whereas some would sooner or later begin to urinate or merely stand there without participation (in time, I discovered that these were the older ones), others kicked up their hind legs as if they were possessed. I resorted to this mode of satisfaction for approximately two months; then it began to disgust me and I stopped.

Long before this time, and for years thereafter, I loved to watch animals mate, especially dogs, and was never able to explain the phenomenon of coupling in dogs, all the more so as the young men and women on the farm never laughed as much at the sight of dogs mating as at the coupling.

I was extremely fond of dogs, especially very little or very big ones. To my parents' great dismay, I accepted pups as presents from all the farmhands who were dog owners. What I liked so much about them was the fact that their snouts appeared so human to me. I was always annoyed when, in time, they grew longer, as I preferred round, nicely shaped forms to elongated, rectangular ones. Thus, I also rounded off the corners of many a toy or farm machine with my penknife. This is, of course, another proof of my attachment to Mother and the great pleasure I experienced as a child when I touched her breasts or suckled them. It just occurred to me that I always petted those pups on their heads and snouts with a slightly cupped hand and that the moistness was decidedly pleasurable. There is an analogy here to the motions of an infant when it touches its mother's breasts with its hands.

Since my parents urged me never to stray far from home, I considered it a bit of luck that I had to have boards made at the cartwright's to mount my butterfly collection and on this pretext asked permission to go there. I was happiest when I was allowed to plane the little boards myself, but, naturally, I got nowhere. The cartwright had a beautiful daughter, so I promised to give him tobacco and then waited anxiously for any chance to steal some from Father's locked drawer. When Father went away one day, I asked Mother for the keys to the house, under some pretense, and proceeded to try the drawer to his desk. By sheer chance, one of the keys fit perfectly and the drawer opened. All manner of secret things peered out at me. I filled an envelope from an unopened tin of Turkish tobacco and then began to acquaint myself with the contents of the drawer. The first thing I discovered was an album with pictures of beautiful naked women, marvelous nude models. The effect this had on me is not hard to guess. The next thing I found was a book entitled *The Marriage Counselor*. I was almost in a fever as I grabbed the book, shut the drawer, and rushed out into the garden where I began reading. As I read through the book, which was about 150 (?) pages, I had an erection, my heart was pounding, and my face was flushed. When I saw the well-known drawing of a child in the womb, a feeling of sudden illumination came over me, and I was happy that my assumptions had been correct. I had always envisioned it that way and no other, although it did seem silly to me that the child lay inside with its head pointing downward. I was also very stimulated by the equally well-known cross section of the uterus, vagina, and rectum. The hair on the labia fascinated me and I could have sat there looking at it for days if I hadn't been driven by the fear that Father might possibly arrive home earlier than expected. I put the book back into the drawer and firmly resolved to study it thoroughly at the next opportunity, especially since there was no difficulty in getting at it with the help of the spare key.

But the child proposes and the father disposes! The next day was to prove just how correct this saying is. Father had, of course, immediately noticed the missing tobacco, but suspected me least of all. He called me in and asked whether I had taken the tobacco. Since I had come to resent his incessant strictness and thrashings, I answered with a clear no. After some close questioning, Father was just about to let me go when Mother entered, holding in her hand the *corpus delicti*; namely, a cigarette-rolling device which she had found in my jacket pocket. That settled it. I received a good beating and slinked off into the garden, without shedding a tear. The beating didn't bother me, I was used to that, but being betrayed by Mother confused me completely. She had delivered me into Father's clutches! I could not get over it, nor did I ever forgive her.

In the summer of that year, we were visited by the female cousin with whom I had once torn off the tail of the hobbyhorse, along with her governess and her little brother, who was Robert's age. Naturally, I fell in love with her straightaway and felt bitter when she preferred my brother to me.

During that time, I also learned to ride, which I enjoyed very much, and went hunting—in secret, of course. Our estate included a fish pond of approximately five hundred hectares which offered a magnificent opportunity for hunting wild ducks and otters. My father had always been a keen hunter, and a Sunday never passed without the gentlemen from the nearby county seat and county court coming to visit us, usually with their wives. Since I would have liked to participate in everything but was forbidden to go hunting, for fear of some mishap, I struck out independently. The employees whose task it was to protect the fish pond from poachers were equipped with guns and I bribed one of them with fifty heller to row out with me. He agreed, and how proud I was when, after missing several times, I saw a wild duck lying in the water, dead. But now what? I could not admit that I had shot it myself and therefore persuaded the keeper to accompany me home and claim that he had shot the duck. That was the way it started, and from then on, I went hunting frequently, although only in Father's absence. Later, I succeeded in convincing Father to allow me to shoot occasionally with him. How happy I was when I received permission. Soon I was lord of the hunting grounds and could even keep up with the hunting parties. Eating the game which I had shot and which was so beautifully prepared by Mother was my greatest pleasure for quite some time.

My physical development was incredibly rapid. I simply shot upward and Mother would say with pride, "He is almost as tall as I."

At approximately eleven and a half, I had intercourse for the first time. It was with a cook who had been hired from someone in town. She was the first to teach me the thrusting motion necessary for ejaculation and at that time it occurred so quickly and unexpectedly that I was frightened and thought it had been an accident. From then on, I had intercourse almost every day for years—it was always in the afternoon, when my parents were napping. Later, I tried it at night, too, whenever Father was away from home. I gradually grew so daring that I attempted it when Father was home, and that almost ended unhappily. The room where I slept was adjacent to my parents' bedroom but had a door to the corridor and from there one could enter the servants' room. A few minutes after Father turned off his light, I got up, dressed only in a nightshirt, went to the door, and slowly opened it. Suddenly, I heard someone strike a match; I rushed back into bed, pretending to be asleep. Father came to my room, found the door open, "woke" me, and asked if I had been outside. Naturally, I acted as if I had just been startled out of a deep slumber.

Since the open door remained an unsolved riddle, Father went out, alarmed the night watchmen, and set out to find the "thieves," armed, of course, with his revolver. My heart was pounding from the shock and I was kept awake by the horrible thought of what Father would have done if he had caught me. After that, I prudently discontinued experiments of this sort.

Now I should like to relate the actual incident to which this chapter owes its title.

Since H. could not be engaged for the next school year because he had to enter military service, a search was begun for another tutor. H. recommended one of his fraternity brothers, who had just completed his first state examination and who, as he told us, would teach us sports properly, for, although small in stature, he was an excellent athlete. (How important to us that seemed at the time!)

S. came to us at the beginning of the academic year and proved to be an affable, pleasant young man who devoted himself to us wholeheartedly. He was an outstanding dancer and soon taught me this art. During our working hours he was strict, although not as severe as his predecessor.

In the fall, Grandmother came to visit for a few weeks, and after that, a period of three or four months passed, partly in interesting work and partly in hours of happy activity. In the winter, we went bobsledding every day, even in the coldest weather, took glorious walks, and always came home hungry to Mother, who awaited us with hot coffee and big, thick slices of bread spread with drippings or honey. My mother looked after S. with the same care she gave us; it even seemed that she was trying to mother him. Strangely, Father did not notice this, whereas he usually saw the dark side in much more innocent cases.

This seems to be the right place to embark upon a detailed description of Mother's physical and emotional constitution, and so I shall attempt it with the greatest possible objectivity.

At the time in question, Mother was thirty-three years old, her build was slender, her face round, with a beautiful, gentle profile and delicate features. She had thick, jet-black hair which fell in natural waves all the way to her knees whenever she let it down. Her eyes were also black, her nose small and straight, her complexion as white as snow. As the daughter of a merchant, she had been raised in the city. When she was two years old, her father died, but her mother soon married an extremely kind, intelligent man, whom she loved very much as a stepfather. Her brother had left home for America at age eighteen and had never been heard from again. Her upbringing in her parents' home was in keeping with the customs of those and of present times; in other words, she had waited for a man. At the age of nineteen, she married Father, who loved her dearly to the day of her death, although she suffered indescribably because of his bad temper and jealousy. Her infinite kindness far outweighed any other less appealing traits and also made her adored by friends and acquaintances and especially by my paternal grandfather, who always protected her from Father's outbursts. The postcards and letters she wrote to us during her journeys (which I have kept) will bear out the fact that she was an exceptionally loyal and self-sacrificing mother to whom her children meant everything.

S. began to court her. He arranged for pleasant drives and seemed to become bolder as he grew aware of the situation at home and also of the fact that she fancied him. I am not quite sure just how the developing affair began, because I noticed nothing. I first became conscious of the situation and began to keep track of it one afternoon when Father was asleep and I saw my mother going into the tutor's room. The feelings I had at the time were partly erotic curiosity and partly fear (fear that Father might wake up—I thought no further). From that day on, I constantly played the role of monitor and pursuer, but also that of defender, in the event of a possible surprise by my father. I cannot explain to myself the reasons for my behavior. Either it was my unconscious hatred of Father or the sexual titillation of being party to such a horrible secret that prevented me from telling Father anything. I think both these elements were equally responsible for my behavior. The relationship grew deeper; not a day passed on which they didn't seek and find an opportunity to be alone. This situation lasted about three months. Their afternoon meetings were limited to just a few minutes and I never thought of the possibility of their having sexual intercourse. One day, however, I became certain of it. Father had gone out at about six o'clock and stayed away for a long while. I spent the entire time waiting in the foyer, struggling to decide whether to disturb them or to report it to Father. Some very vague feeling restrained me from doing either. Then, when Mother (oh, what a terrible ring that word now has!) came out of the room, which I could see was completely darkened, with flushed cheeks and a wild, darting look in her eyes, I knew for sure it had happened, although I had no way of telling whether or not for the first time. I stood in a corner, cowering behind a cabinet, with tears streaming down my face. I wanted to run to her but could not do it, to the great misfortune of us all. I am still deeply convinced that seeing me at this point would have brought her to her senses, even though belatedly, and saved us our mother as well as Father his wife. This would have been the only possible salvation! Just what held me back at that moment I cannot say, but at the same time I began to feel pity for Father, and gritting my teeth, I crept away. I was then eleven and a half or twelve years old.

Nothing had changed in our daily life. I cannot recall any scenes of jealousy between my parents during this period.

Shortly after Christmas, Father went away for three weeks. During that time I had the most horrible and repulsive experiences imaginable, which buried themselves deep in my thoughts and emotions.

During Father's absence, Mother slept with Grandmother in the back room at the end of the hall; after it came our room, then the dining room, and then the tutor's—one connected to the other. The very first night (I hadn't shut an eye from excitement), I heard Mother get out of bed—even now disgust seems to be strangling me—and tiptoe through our bedroom in her nightgown. Soon I heard his door open and close partially. Then all was quiet. I jumped out of bed and crept after her, freezing, with my teeth chattering from cold and fear and horror. Slowly I made my way to the door of his room. It was ajar. I stood there and listened. Oh, the frightful memories that drag each recollection of my mother down into the dust, that soil my image of her with muck and filth! Must I go into details? My pen refuses to obey me. No, it is I myself refusing with all my might, yet I want to, I will, I must if I am to do justice to the title of this section.

I heard them kissing, whispering, and the horrible creaking of the bed in which my mother lay. Ten feet away stood her own child, a witness to her disgrace. Suddenly, there was quiet. Probably I had made some sound in my excitement. Then his soothing voice, and then, then again, again—oh!

Oh, composure, peace! What a superhuman effort it takes to view this shattering tragedy "objectively"! What mockery! What an undertaking! All I remember of that catastrophic night is that I wanted to rush into the room, but was held back by the thought: they might kill you! I recalled having read that a lover will kill anyone who disturbs him. With a head full of bizarre fantasies I crept back to bed, without hope of consolation, my youthful spirit broken! For the first time, a deep feeling of misfortune and of having been abandoned overcame me.

And so it happened night after night. I followed her to his door and waited there until morning. Gradually I became accustomed to it! My horror gave way to erotic feelings. Once I even considered breaking in on them and demanding that she have intercourse with me too (shame!), threatening that otherwise I would tell Father. During the final few days, I visited the cook regularly.

When Father was away, Mother and S. made practically no secret of their relationship. During the day they danced and laughed, while Grandmother watched their frolicking. Today I must agree with Father in his accusation that Grandmother was the matchmaker. She certainly at least encouraged the illicit activity.

Days passed, months went by, and when vacation time came, S. left our house without Father's having noticed anything. During the summer he even mentioned on several occasions that S. should come back the following year—but Mother was strictly against it. Apparently, her better traits and her remorse had gained the upper hand. The vacation passed very pleasantly with visits from our relatives. Everything could have continued along the same old lines, but fate decided otherwise.

At the beginning of the school year, Father engaged a university student who was a nice, sincere person, although not quite as young and lighthearted as S. Mother was so curt to him that Father asked her on several occasions why she was treating him that way.

At Christmas, Father and Mother went away for two weeks to visit an uncle, to whom, as I later heard, their marriage seemed very harmonious; they appeared to be fonder of each other than ever before, with the exception of one ugly incident. Mother and Uncle had gone into the bedroom to look at the new furnishings while the rest of the company remained in the dining room. Father then actually began to suspect her of having a relationship with his own brother and reviled her for not even having the decency to abstain from intercourse "in broad daylight" and "standing up."

Upon returning home, Mother was either possessed by the devil again or had been plunged into a depression by Father's unfortunate behavior—in short, several weeks later I noticed that she lingered in the dining room with the tutor for a long time.

Nothing serious had happened as yet when the catastrophe suddenly erupted with full intensity.

It was evening and Robert and I were sitting in our room, from which one door led to the dining room, another to my parents' bedroom, while a third opened onto the hallway. Father had gone to the stables. Mother had been in the kitchen, and the tutor in his room. Suddenly the door from the hall was thrown open and in rushed Father. He was pale, there was a wild vacant look in his eyes, and he was wearing a hat, coat, and rubber boots covered with dung. He was quickly followed by Mother, who was also pale and trembling. Father screamed at her in a crazed, gasping voice: "What were you doing with him alone in the hall just now, you whore? Tell me! Why did he jump back a few steps when I came in!? Why did he jump back, I ask you? Now off to the bedroom with you for an accounting!" And he dragged her into the bedroom while we remained in our room, terrified of what the outcome would be. I knew my father's temper and expected to hear a shot any second, but nothing of the sort happened. There was only (!) the sound of someone being pushed around and landing on the bed. Then came Father's voice, full of rage: "You tell me everything or I'll murder you—every detail of all the love affairs you've had up to now." Mother swore that there had been nothing between her and the tutor, but it did her little good. Shortly thereafter, Father entered our room and closed the door. There were beads of perspiration on his forehead as he called us both to come to him and tell everything we knew. Threateningly, he demanded an answer. I trembled as I said that I knew nothing about our present tutor but that I had been a witness to Mother's relationship with S. from beginning to end. It is impossible to describe how Father went rigid when I told him. He pressured me to tell him everything, and I did—unfortunately, too late. Haltingly, in broken sentences, I related how I had listened behind the door but had not dared to do anything, for fear of being killed. Suddenly we heard a deep groan in the other room. Father rushed in, and then we heard his voice, sobbing: "Egleia,* what have you done? I promise you by everything that is holy—all is forgiven—but tell me, tell me, what did you take? Oh, God, Egleia, for the children's sake, don't die—I forgive you!"

We ran into their bedroom and saw Mother in the dark, writhing on the bed. She had taken poison, Lysol!!!

Father threw open the window and poured an emetic into her, which helped. Mother vomited up everything—but nevertheless had to remain in bed for a time with her stomach burned, her mouth raw.

And now a period of suffering began for Father, Mother, and also for us children. It was but a prelude to Mother's tragic death and Father's destiny to follow her after only a short time.

Father loved Mother far too much ever to have been capable of separating from her, and, besides, he wanted to avoid a scan-

---

*Reich's mother's name was Cäcilie. Egleia may have been a special name used by her husband. [Eds.]

dal. His intention was to try to forgive her, to try to live with her, if only to ensure that the children would have a mother.

The following months were full of confusion, horrible situations and complications which obscured every possible solution to the problem. Even now, I despair at having to describe the period between January and October 1910. To be capable of understanding the spiritual battles waged at that time, one would require a complete, unbiased knowledge of the soul.

Where Father got the idea of demanding that L., our tutor, should ask Mother to forgive him in my presence and avow that he had not had any "intentions," I was never able to understand.

The next step Father took was to send us to the Gymnasium in town and dismiss the tutor. I was sent to board with a childless couple. The husband had been a failure as a student. His family was extremely well-to-do and in his youth he had wasted vast sums of money and had then been forced to become an insurance agent. His wife was young and pleasant. We were treated well there and stayed with them for four years.

Robert was not sent into town at the same time as I, for he was just about to take the entrance examinations for the Gymnasium. Father hired a somewhat older student to tutor him until the summer.

At the same time, Father and Mother had gone into town to see Grandmother, to whom Father told the whole story. How incredible is the manner in which she received the news, and the advice she gave: "What has happened has happened—you must make your peace now, and eventually all will be well."* Father

---

*[Added in 1944] How logical and rational! How mistaken my ideas were in 1919. The situation has now become clear to me: what Mother did was perfectly all right! My betrayal, which cost her her life, was an act of revenge: she had betrayed me to Father when I stole the tobacco for the cartwright, and in return I then betrayed *her*! What a tragedy! I wish my mother were alive today so that I could make good for the crime I committed in those days, thirty-five years ago. I have set up a picture of that noble woman so that I can look at it over and over again. What a noble creature, this woman—my mother! May my life's work make good for my misdeed. In view of my father's brutality, she was perfectly right!

seemed to have had second thoughts about Grandmother's innocence in the unfortunate affair, for he began to ask questions
of us and of Grandmother, too, surreptitiously. And then he
discovered that Mother and S. had also met at Grandmother's
house. When I informed him, to complete matters, that one day
Grandmother, Mother, S., and I had passed a pharmacy and
that S. had gone in, soon to return to them laughing with a red
package in his hand, Father no longer doubted that Grandmother
had been an accomplice, for the little package had contained
condoms. Later, Mother also confessed that she had spoken to
Grandmother about divorcing Father and marrying S., whereupon Father forbade her to visit Grandmother under any circumstances. He himself wrote her a nasty letter accusing her of
matchmaking and pandering and calling her an old whore, a
shrew, etc. (and rightly so!). Grandmother complained to our
uncle, and he, in turn, threatened to sue for libel (which he
prudently refrained from doing). As for S., Father had various
plans in mind for him. At first, he wanted to seek him out and
shoot him. Next, he proposed that Mother force S. to marry
her, which she adamantly refused to do. (S. seemed to have
disappeared from the face of the earth—I never saw him again.)
On another occasion, Father unleashed his entire fury on Mother
and exonerated S. of all blame by claiming that any young man
would gladly have entered into such a relationship.

His sudden temper and his anguish repeatedly gained the upper hand. In attacks of senseless rage which occurred almost
daily, he would beat Mother mercilessly. Then he decided to
rent an apartment for Mother and us in town, while he continued
to live in the country. Had he followed this plan, much would
have been resolved; above all, it would have prevented both
their deaths. But his jealousy had a fatal effect. Mother constantly implored him on bended knee to forgive her and threatened to hang herself at any attempt by Father to separate from
her. She agreed to live with us in town, promised not to cast a
glance at anyone and just be with the children. (Secretly, I am
sure, the poor woman hoped that time, even if it was years,

would heal Father's wound and that he would forgive her completely.) But the minute she expressed her agreement to such a plan Father started screaming that all she wanted was to be alone in town so that she could begin other affairs without interference. He, however, was willing neither to disgrace himself and his children in such a way nor to do her the "favor." Thus, his jealousy again kept him from following the only correct path.

Every time Robert and I saw each other, he told me how horribly Mother suffered. It happened every day, especially in the evening. Father would begin, and go on and on. At first, he would cry and bemoan his fate. Gradually, he would become so involved in his own rage that he physically mistreated Mother and called her hideous names, until she was left cowering in some corner or had fled into the garden. During that period, her face, hands, and body bore the marks of his rage.

When Father and Mother came into town, scenes took place regularly as we passed the clubhouse and reading room of L.'s fraternity. When we arrived at the spot, he would shout at her that she should go inside to her beloved, where she could surrender to him and his fellows and maybe even earn a pretty penny. But just as the unfortunate woman tolerated his blows at home, she bore the verbal abuse here. Her unearthly patience convinced me that the perpetual avowals of her love for Father were not empty phrases, or else she would not have found it necessary to bear such suffering.

During short visits at home and especially during vacations, I was able to verify the indescribable scenes. There was no end to Father's new ideas. He linked the most remote incidents or memories to Mother's infidelity. For example, he began to doubt that Robert was really his son, because Mother had been away at a spa shortly before his conception. Once, when my cousin was visiting, she had rashly kidded Mother in Father's presence about some "gentleman in black" at a spa. The discussion of this incident (like all others) ended with physical abuse. Now Father suspected everyone; once, for example, he considered the night watchman who had held the light for Mother on her way down into the cellar. H., our first tutor, was also included. Of course, all these accusations were utterly unfounded, for (and I am thoroughly convinced of this) Mother had been a perfectly faithful spouse to Father up until the day she met S. After the incident had been exposed, she loved him as dearly as before.

She bore these accusations and the abuse with meekness. Never did she contradict him or try to defend herself and only rarely asked him to be a little patient and show consideration for the children. Whereupon he would ask, naturally while beating her, whether she had shown consideration for the children as she wandered through the house at night to the bed of her disgrace. He was correct, but under such circumstances the idea of living with her should never even have crossed his mind. *He had no right to dispose of her life!*

One day, when I was back in town, a servant came and summoned me to a hotel. Mother was lying in a room, her face puffy, her eyes swollen from crying. She begged me to help her, for *physically* she could no longer endure the situation: she said she would poison herself again if things did not change soon. She would not hear of a divorce. After several days, Father took her home again.

Summer vacation came and I went home for two months. Needless to say, the old situation continued. During the day there was often an excellent understanding between them, but at night there were always ghastly scenes and ever-increasing violence. Mother had become completely numb and apathetically allowed the blows to rain down upon her. Several weeks later, she tried to poison herself with sublimate, but, owing to her strong constitution, she had only internal burns and had to spend several weeks in bed. During this period, Father was entirely different again, as if nothing had happened, as if he had never mistreated her so hideously. But she had hardly recovered when his personality changed and he began all over again. Soon Mother lost our support, for we turned away from her and no longer made any effort to protect her from Father's assaults as we had done before. Yes, one day I actually raised my voice to her for some minor reason.

Thus, the poor woman was driven to death like a hunted animal by her husband and children! None of us saw any way to remedy the situation. We all suffered—and she most of all. I do not hesitate to say that in those few months she more than atoned for what she had done.

The only members of the family who knew of the catastrophe were Mother's uncle, Grandmother, and Uncle Isidor. Not one of them raised so much as a finger to help us. Another uncle of ours, Arnold, would perhaps have taken action, had he known. But Father did not want to tell him, because he assumed—and correctly so—that the matter would travel to our uncle's wife and with her, or through her, to all our other relatives and friends.

The end of vacation drew near, and with it the day that Robert would also go into town to live. Mother said nothing, but what torment it must have caused her to think that she would now be completely alone and at the mercy of Father's rage.

We had already been in town for a month (September) and had not seen Mother. Toward the end of the month—it was on a Monday—Father paid us his usual visit and drove back home in the evening. Tuesday afternoon, however, he returned and informed us that Mother was extremely ill—she had taken poison again, but this time she was not going to survive. He had come into town to fetch us and a doctor. We three shed silent tears. There was no comfort to be had; no word was spoken. We all knew that it had to be that way. On Monday, Mother had poisoned herself while Father was away (it was impossible to discover what she had taken). Toward evening, she had hemorrhaged and was being looked after by the steward's wife, who thought it was a miscarriage. When Father arrived home on Monday, Mother was lying in bed and asked him to forgive her. She had had to do it, she said, but she wanted to see the children one last time.

Father immediately sent for the doctor (an old acquaintance of his) and told him everything. The doctor held out little hope and recommended that a famous internist from Czernowitz be called in because of the imminent danger of uremia due to kidney dysfunction. Father had therefore gone back to town the same day and asked the doctor to come out.

But this physician also pronounced the case hopeless. He said that only an operation could save her. However the operation would have to be done immediately and he had no instruments with him; she might not survive being transported into town. How horrible it was to hear this. We all stayed awake that night. Mother was fully conscious. At about two o'clock in the morning she said, "Only one more hour!" How I shuddered at the words! I was kneeling next to her; Father had buried his head in the pillows and constantly whimpered, "Forgive me, forgive me!" She lived through another day. The evening came. Robert was so tired that he had lain down in bed. Father and I waited. Only the doctor and the steward were actually in the room where Mother lay; they did not want to let us in for fear that our frightful state would disturb Mother.

At approximately two o'clock, Mother called for us. Father and I rushed in and fell to our knees at her bedside. Never had I seen her so beautiful! There she lay, with cheeks flushed and her wavy hair loosened. She gazed at us with dreamy eyes and placed both her hands on our heads. Then she asked to see Robert, who was awakened and brought in. Only the four of us were in the room, united once again—and all was forgiven, but alas, it was too late! Father cried and sobbed, whispering the same words over and over: "Egleia, forgive me, do not die!" Again and again, in a monotone. He appeared to have lost his senses. Mother could only whisper, "Leo,* I was always true to you—it was only that once—forgive me now—Willy and Robert are your children—be good to them for me!" And thus we waited

---

*Reich's father's name was Leon, but Leo is the name that appears in this manuscript. [Eds.]

for death to take her. Oh, how beautiful she was as she lay there. "Just as she looked on her wedding day," Father said later. We kissed her left hand as she held her right hand to her chest. She shed silent tears. The last we saw was that she tried to raise her right hand to her mouth to wipe away some saliva. Her hand came to a halt just below her chin. Mother was dead.

But the fact that my Mother had died, as sad as it was in itself, and under such circumstances, overwhelmed me less with grief than with fascination at a novel situation. Mother was the first person I had seen die. Yes, I must admit that I felt a certain pride in having the right to be called an orphan. Later on, when I began to ponder life and death, mankind and its lot, I reached the conclusion that the religious ceremonies which automatically ensue when a person dies run their strict course perhaps for the very purpose of suppressing feelings of mourning (if not directly, then indirectly). By this, I mean the genuine mourning which forces one to turn away and be alone and which I experienced only once, later in life, at the death of a friend. As a rule, it is suppressed, or rather masked by all that convention requires, the handshaking, the thanking for sympathy shown, arranging for the burial, etc. This can have a therapeutic effect if it relieves one of the necessity of feigning grief before *oneself*. But I would not like the task of deciding whether the other necessity, namely of exhibiting grief to the outside world, is any easier, especially when that grief is the genuine expression of an inner loss.

When Mother died, I felt not even a trace of inner grief. On the day after she died, when she was still lying on her deathbed, I charged into the room amidst all the wailing women who surrounded her, and drew back the sheet so that her face was visible. I acted as if I had been irresistibly compelled to do this, but was thoroughly taken aback when I saw her marble countenance. A new feeling I had never known before arose within me, no thoughts crossed my mind, but I marveled for the first time in my life that a human being could look that way and be physically present without breathing. Her motionless breasts made me feel oppressed—the breasts which had once given me life, nurtured me. Later in life, I always knew that I really loved a girl when I wanted to kiss her breasts more than her lips, when, with my head resting upon her breasts, I experienced the peacefulness that was nowhere else to be found. I cannot recall ever having kissed the breasts of a prostitute, despite the fact that this type of woman played no small part in my life. Breasts which are round, full, supple, do not sag, and have a rosy-white hue are the most beautiful part of a woman. That is why I like poems that extol women's breasts with chaste but sensuous desire, for no yearning within me will ever be as strong as that for a woman's breast upon which to rest my head. Later I experienced many a night in which I abstained from intercourse but found a complete substitute for it by resting my head on a girl's breast and pressing close to her body. Granted, my desire for intercourse was great (although by no means exclusive of all else), but a vague feeling that, through coitus, I might somehow lose my beloved emotionally made me continue reluctantly to bear the abstinence. I can only say that the mother breast assumed substantial importance for me, although I do not remember ever paying particular attention to the actual breasts of my own mother. I did, however, pay ample attention to those of other women—even in earliest childhood.

When I left the room where her remains were lying, a feeling of shame arose within me—I had exposed Mother before other people; somehow I had bared myself—bared myself through Mother, or with her. I cannot specify more clearly what exactly I mean by this. But here I must mention one thing; namely, that among my later character traits, emotional masochism was far from being unobtrusive. When I found myself in dire material need after Father's death, I quite enjoyed the role of martyr. This was one aspect of my attitude toward poverty, and I feel that this type of masochistic satisfaction is responsible for a major part of one's ability to sustain courage and not lose heart when times are bad.

I did not complain to others, even allowed them to believe that I was well-to-do, and then was impressed with myself for "suffering in silence." After all, Mother had suffered a lot without complaining. Father always said I shared the traits of my mother's family, so how can it be surprising that I did actually have a womanly streak? Subsequently, this was to cause great unhappiness, though much happiness as well, and a certain lofty detachment in the realm of my emotions and my love life, in music, in my reading and theatergoing. But all this came about later, and only after a period marked by complete emotional brutality and calculation.

When the burial was over, Father and we children went to the house of one of his brothers who lived in a small town several hours away by train. Oh, what melodramatic scenes there were—that sham emotionalism which longs for display. I found it distasteful even then, but I joined in, nevertheless. A peculiar set of circumstances then brought it about that, only a few days after Mother's death, we laid our offerings on the altars of whoredom in dance halls and honky-tonks: Father, my uncle, his son, and I, who was almost fourteen years old at the time but had matured quickly, physically and emotionally, far beyond my years. It was then that I became acquainted with my cousin, a well-developed girl thirteen years old, whose parents both claimed that she looked very much like me. Naturally, I fell in love with her immediately and stayed in love—I can hardly believe it myself—for seven years, long after I realized that we had no intellectual ties. Today I simply cannot understand how our dear fathers (with all the experience they must have gathered with me in honky-tonks) could smile at our "love affair" and found it amusing when I kissed the girl in their presence, when I embraced her, and when my behavior was so unmistakably motivated by the desire to have intercourse. Belief in the absolute innocence of fourteen-year-olds blinded them completely.

My cousin had been given an old-fashioned upbringing, had learned to stammer a few words in French (I think she still does today) and to pound on the piano, despite the fact that she had no ear for music or the slightest musical ability. Often I caught myself wishing that she would desist, for I did not enjoy having my impressions of a piece of music ruined. And yet I loved her! I loved her, despite the fact that she couldn't dance and was very ungraceful, whereas I (until I was twenty) found an outlet for my agility in the enjoyment of dancing; I loved her, despite the fact that she could not follow the involved thread of my conversation and asked stupid questions; I loved her, despite the fact that she bored me! Perhaps this is only the impression I have today. But one thing is certain: I was crazy for someone to love and the first girl who crossed my path would have to do. The fact that one can kiss a cousin and not be punished also contributed greatly. I wanted to love, I needed an object for my daydreams and longings, and the way my love object felt about this—or about me—soon mattered little. Only when I had reason to fear that I might lose her, when her marriage and the candidates were discussed (she was like a young cow which was stuffed with piano lessons, French, and Marlitt novels before being led to the bull), or when I had to return to my town because of school, only then did love flame up wildly within me, and I am ashamed of the letters I sent her during the long months we were apart—letters I wrote only because I was writing to *her*, a girl who never understood them. If I wrote about my plans for the future, she would reply: "I am sure you know best!" If I complained of being alone and yearning for love, she didn't answer at all. Later, when she was eighteen, and I asked her why she had not replied to one of these letters, she said: "But such things are not discussed in writing!" For a moment I thought: Would she prefer the real thing? But then I realized that *she* certainly would not! (Sex and vitality of the spirit bear a relationship to each other, a relationship which, as such, could be verified through facts and examples, although it is otherwise still extremely obscure. Well, she was completely sexless!) I shudder at the thought that I might have fallen for her when I recall how years later, at a time when she must already have been worrying about becoming an old maid (possibly with a lapdog), she would describe for hour after monotonous hour, ad infinitum, how it would be when she was married, how she would greet me when

I came to visit, and other such nonsense. This clearly illustrated her ever-growing concern that she might not be *cared for* (what a telling expression!).

While the platonic (idealistic) aspect of my sexuality was fixated in this rut, my eroticism (the sensual component) went thoroughly wild in brothels, stairwells, and cellars. Before I had ever been in a brothel, I pictured them as large halls with many mirrors and beds, in which naked women lay, legs spread to receive man after man. This fantasy was accompanied by curiosity to experience it and by a vague sense of disgust. (I must say that this picture was not far off the mark when compared to the brothels I saw at the front during my military service.)

The first time I went to a brothel, at age fifteen, I submitted to it like a test. After a spree that had lasted well into the night and left me half drunk, I was led down a dark, narrow street. There I saw a building several stories high, with windows that were darkened but glowing through blinds in many different shades of yellow, green, and red. This aroused my curiosity, rather than my sexual expectations, to the point of a tickling physical sensation in the genital area. I entered, or rather was dragged into, the "salon." It seemed to me at the time that it was full of women from another world—no, from a play, or more likely an opera ballet which I had once seen. They were sitting, standing, dancing, singing, jabbering. Someone was assigned to me and I suddenly felt my hands between soft, warm thighs. I forgot everything. I think that, to the amusement of everyone present, I rushed at her in the "salon." I can no longer remember that coitus—I awoke out of a half sleep and hungered for the woman again. She had long since recognized me as a beginner and literally drove me out of my mind with her hysterical writhing to enhance the pleasure (or perhaps because a prostitute can fully realize her sexuality and femininity only with a fifteen-year-old). Later I often thought back to the staggering intensity of this affect and could never explain how it had been possible that I, who had been having intercourse for three years, and quite regularly, could lose myself so completely. Was it the atmosphere, the clothing, the red light, the provocative nakedness, the smell of whores—I don't know! I was pure sensual lust; *I* had ceased to be—I was all penis! I bit, scratched, thrust, and the girl had quite a time with me! I thought I would have to crawl inside her. In short, I had lost myself! I slept until the sun was up, and when I awoke, she was lying next to me, naked. Only then did I take a closer look at her. A young, frail creature was lying there in bed with me. Not even for a second did it occur to me that she was a "whore." I kissed her on the lips and she awoke. We embraced again and then I left. For the first time, I did not have the bleak feeling one experiences after intercourse with unwashed maids, half dressed, on the tops of barrels, in cellars, or wherever. I had asked her to belong to me alone, said I would pay for everything, but when I returned that evening and requested her, I was informed that she was working at the moment. I foamed at the mouth, dashed out the door, and did not see the inside of a brothel again for the next three years! But I succumbed to excessive masturbation. My school friends had told me of the dangers of masturbation and demonstrated with pictures, but I continued stubbornly, despite the nagging worries in my heart. I was afraid of becoming impotent, for an older cousin had informed me that at eighteen I would no longer be capable of intercourse! But still I continued to masturbate. Daydreams flourished like weeds. I had difficulty concentrating in class, for I was dreaming, dreaming with my eyes open, dreaming when I wrote mathematical formulas on the blackboard, dreaming when I was to recite German poetry or literary passages! I was one of the best pupils in the class without really exerting myself. Father was pressing me to get honors. But I didn't care about Father; he was a bother and annoyed me, although my relationship with him gradually improved over what it had been while Mother was alive. I had little contact with my classmates. I read a lot, devoured both belles lettres and scientific writings, improvised on the piano for hours, and gave lessons to add to my pocket money. I worked, played, brooded, dreamed, and masturbated! I withdrew from the world and let my classmates go their own ways, for their prurient talk and actions and their smoking disgusted me! There was only one with whom I maintained a friendship over the years, the one who later died. Depressive states began to grow more frequent, I would brood about women and about love. The woman I married was to be someone very special. At night I would lie awake, my eyes burning—thinking, thinking, brooding, yearning—and then finally masturbate! Soon I found it was actually not pleasurable but unpleasurable, I did it compulsively! At first I thought: Save your energy for the magnificent woman you will have one day; but then I would begin to doubt: You will never find her anyway, so what difference does it make? I could not look anyone in the eye. I lied, for I had to lie, and I yearned for a woman to whom I could confide everything that troubled my spirit. Every lie I was forced to tell was followed by severe self-reproach. I both hated and loved myself. I went to the theater often and will never forget the impression which *The Cardinal* and *Oedipus Rex* made upon me. I loved the ballet, fell in love with the prima donna of the opera, and greatly admired the actor who played Oedipus and who, as I was later informed, was homosexual. Homosexuality was a mystery to me (just as the brothels had been), but with a negative connotation. I had often slept in the same bed with a friend of mine, but there had never been any genital contact. I was in love with his sister because of her glorious, long, blond hair. After the theater, I would always accompany her home the roundabout way and then had to make excuses, saying that the play had lasted so long. She somehow reminded me of Dahn's *Felicitas* and Storm's "Aquis Submersus," which had made an especially deep impression on me. C.P.A.S., those four secret letters on the boy's picture which stood for: *culpa patris aquis submersus.* Ewers excited me; Wilde delighted me, although Sudermann did not; Spielhagen left me completely cold except for the novel where the hero drowns himself. I couldn't stand the classic poets, but I loved Schiller's *Ghost-Seer.* I read Hauff's *Tales* over and over, loved the Russian writers and despised the French, was enthusiastic about Wallace's *Ben Hur* (before reading the book, I had thought the title meant "son of a whore"), and thus found a means of approach to the magnificent Strindberg, whose biography (son of a maid, etc.) I read at a time when my entire soul was one large wound. At age sixteen, I began to devour legends of Christ (*Quo Vadis*, etc.) and began to pray again, despite the fact that I had been a confirmed atheist for eight years. I cursed my father (as I also did frequently in later life) because he had locked me away both at home and in school and had not allowed me to play with any other children of my own age until I was eleven. I grew serious and moody before my time, and as a result I now crave the pleasures of life. My father barred my way; he infected me with his ambition and caused my problems. Everything which other people simply take in their stride represents a tiring process of searching and finding for me. I had to bring home honors, play the piano for strangers I disliked, because he had doled out the money for a teacher. I had to show my proficiency in French; again, because *he* was paying for the lessons. ("Am I supposed to spend *my* money and not have any pleasure from my children?") And yet he was an intelligent man whom I not only hated but also loved. I was beginning to live exclusively for my dreams and books when a young girl came to live with us, a "high-class" cook. After two weeks, I was having an affair with her. I sensed a new, different, real kind of pleasure and slowly emerged from my shell.

I went on outings, played soccer and tennis, and—I met the sister of a classmate. She was eighteen years old, had a dark complexion, red lips, small feet in dainty shoes, and a graceful body from her slender neck down to her waist and to her lovely hips. It was a humid Sunday morning. From six to eight o'clock, I played tennis with her and her brother. At noon, I was lying on the floor at home, naked, taking a shower every ten minutes. I tried reading Dostoevsky, but my thoughts were elsewhere; my inner unrest was growing. I quickly dressed and set off to visit my friend. When I arrived at his house, all the blinds had been let down. The lovely girl was in the darkened music room, improvising on the piano. The maid, who was just leaving, said, "Only the young lady is at home." Slowly I drew nearer to her. My field of vision grew dark; I saw red and green lights, balls of light, glowing rays, and between them something white; a heavy, strange scent (like gentian) filled my breast; I looked about me for the whiteness. No, I felt it before me—her neck —I bent over and placed a kiss on her half-bare shoulder. She was startled, stretched out her hands—and stayed seated. I wrapped my arms about her from behind and we sank down. But at that very moment I jumped up and ran away as if the devil himself were after me! I never saw her again after that day. She married a customs officer, I was later informed, and bore a child every year! For me, that was not the same woman!

I was once again like a tiger who had smelled blood. I worked like an ox during the day and lay around brothels at night. I felt that I had to find someone or something great. A gradual but ever-increasing disgust for whores arose within me, but to my great dismay, I realized that I could no longer live without a brothel. A horrible struggle ensued. Although I did not make use of the women, I had to visit the brothel every night. I began to observe and reflect on the prostitutes, to compare them to girls of my own class. I paid a young girl, seventeen years old, ten kronen to tell me the story of her life. She began with lies, but I noticed and pressured her until she finally broke down in tears and spewed out her tale of woe. It made me feel desperately unhappy and somehow guilty. I wanted to save her. Her interest was immediately aroused, but then I remembered that I had no financial means and was completely dependent upon Father. I began my withdrawal. And suddenly it occurred to me that I was looking for reasons to avoid fulfilling a duty. I forgot about the girl altogether (she became aware of it) and began to brood about whether or not I was responsible for her. I felt strongly that I was not to blame in her case. Then her attitude changed and she began calling me vile names, saying that I had only wanted to ridicule her. Finally, she threw me out. In a state of utter dejection and confusion, I ran off into a park, entertaining thoughts of suicide and how best to accomplish it. Then another thought shot across my mind: You're lying to yourself! I rushed home, reviling myself for being such a coward, and wrote a one-act play entitled *The Reunion*. The hero (I myself) had seduced a country girl and then deserted her, only to meet up with her again in a brothel. The play ends with the hero being thrown out of the brothel, despised by the whore, who is a better human being than he. Afterwards I felt relieved and fell into a restless sleep, troubled by tormenting dreams in which an owl played a frightening role. The next day I looked very ill. Mrs. X., whom I considered my foster mother and whom I loved very dearly, asked me what was wrong. I pretended to have a severe headache and did not attend school. Instead, I took a two-hour trip out into the country and then went for a long hike. That evening I arrived, tired and despondent, at an inn. I took a room and wrote another one-act play, which I called *The Owl*: the woman whom the hero loves has married another man. Together they visit the hero, who must conceal his distress. After they leave, he espies a horrible creature in the corner of his room; it is an owl. He grabs his Browning to shoot the bird, but the gun goes off aimed at his chest and the hero falls to the floor. This, too, brought me relief. I slept more deeply and dreamlessly than I had for a long time. At sunrise I awoke, took a cold bath, dressed, and felt like a new person. But I was also ashamed of my behavior over the previous few days. When I arrived home at noon, I had news that Father was very ill. Full of horrible fears, I rushed off and found him lying in bed, miserable, pale, and emaciated. I hadn't seen him for several days and at first I did not believe it was he. I went to kiss him as usual, but he held me back, saying that only the day before, he had been informed that he had galloping consumption. If he wanted to survive, he would have to go south immediately; but this he was unable to do. Eight days before, he had lost all his money, due to unfortunate transactions and the bankruptcy of an uncle. But Father had been sickly for a long time, he had been coughing and was exhausted after even the slightest exertion. We had encouraged him to consult a physician, but he had repeatedly postponed it (from a desire to play the invalid—or so it had seemed to me).

In eight days he had lost one quarter of his weight. Vaguely, I sensed the full seriousness of the situation. Again my self-reproach was bitter: I had been wasting time on useless matters while the poor man had been suffering. I resolved to make up for everything. Father had to salvage whatever he could from the financial disaster. Since he was not able to leave his bed, I had him give me instructions and promised to put matters in perfect order. Three precious weeks went by. Fictitious contracts were signed, dirty dealings with hagglers and the vultures who feed on other men's misfortunes went on day after day. Father grew increasingly apathetic. The filth stirred up by the hagglers crushed him completely, for he had always been an honest man and for that very reason had never made a great fortune. He had worked in order to assure his family's well-being and now he was as poor as a beggar, a complete wreck—emotionally because of Mother, physically because of his tuberculosis (which, in turn, was a result of the marital catastrophe he had never recovered from and which had gnawed at him for three years), and financially because of the ruthlessness and dishonesty of a relative who had at one time been very rich and whose bankruptcy had totally devastated hundreds of people, my father among them. I did everything I could to raise a small amount of money for the trip. I ran to our numerous friends, acquaintances, relatives, aunts, uncles, nephews. But how different the world appeared now. I no longer recognized these people! There was outright coldness, shrugging of shoulders, "ands," "ifs," "buts"—disgusting! Where had they gone, all those people who sponged off us when times were better, who proposed the toasts, who exalted my uncle and praised his hospitality? Where did they go? Where are they now? It was the second time in my life that I had been confronted with a puzzling situation, and it was the second time that I was inwardly torn apart. A district attorney who had been a daily guest at our home actually suggested that the insolvent party and his endorsee both be put behind bars, for "reasons of security." Only the insolvent party was then arrested but released on a million-kronen bail (even today, I still cannot figure out how he raised that money), while my father lay dying and I was unable to raise the small sum necessary to save his life; and the chances grew slimmer every day. Finally I succeeded in borrowing a few thousand kronen from the father of a friend. This paid for a six-week stay in a South Tyrol health resort. I accompanied Father on the trip, but shall spare myself a description of the journey. I telegraphed for a comfortable coach which was to be waiting for us at the train station at 2 p.m. It was a magnificent day in May and we were slowly riding up the winding road to a sanatorium three hours away. Father's eyes were glassy and wide open, his cheeks were flushed, and he was taking in deep draughts of the heavenly mountain air. We spoke very little. I had wrapped him in a plaid blanket; he rested his head on my shoulder, closed his eyes, and appeared to doze. I stole a look at him: once he had been so strong, energetic, full of vigor. But how he looked now! And again I felt those indefinable pangs! What a stranger I had remained to him. Had there been no way for us to communicate? I looked back at my childhood, which now appeared in strangely rosy colors. I forgot the beatings I had received so often, forgot his furious look, which had frightened me so horribly, forgot his scolding voice. It was as if everything had been washed away. Memories emerged of joyful games, of gymnastics we shared, bathing, swimming, horseback riding, hunting, memories of the things he had taught us, as well as a thousand other little every-day things: the way he would crawl around the room on all fours, following his afternoon nap, and allow me to ride on his back; the way we mussed his hair. We used to hang onto his strong arms, and he would throw us up and catch us, while Mother stood by, smiling quietly. And I cursed the memory of her, for this was her doing! Just as I had once blamed Father for Mother's death, I now blamed her. But Father was still alive, everything could still turn out well; he would marry. But then a diabolical thought crossed my mind, as it had two years after

Mother's death, when Father had wanted to marry a twenty-year-old girl. This had evoked fantasies within me, and I had romantically envisioned seducing my future stepmother. Father had discussed the matter of his marriage with me at the time, and I had advised him against it, offering other reasons while withholding this one. Now the thought had arisen again, and under such circumstances—I was shocked to recognize the full extent of my own hideousness!

Father awoke and turned to me. "Do you think I'll ever get well?" he asked. "Of course you will, Father!" I replied and drew his attention to the magnificent mountain forests, the sun, and fresh air. He took a deep breath, shivered, and wrapped the blanket around himself. "Do you remember," he asked, "how I talked of dying not long ago and you laughed at me? Well, now I no longer worry about it myself! In surroundings like this, one simply has to recover, and I am already feeling so well!" A convulsive coughing spell interrupted him—I was frightened and had difficulty dismissing my own anxious thoughts.

On my trip home, a telegram reached me, informing me of his death. I drove back with both his brothers and we buried him in Vienna. I have never again seen either my father's or my mother's grave. I was seventeen.

TWO

The Great War
1914–1918

At the outbreak of the war, I was living with my brother on the estate and we were in the midst of harvesting. On July 31, 1914, the general mobilization order came; police posted it everywhere. "War" sounded dangerous, terrible, and strange. No one knew anything except that it had been declared against Serbia. There wasn't one person in six thousand who could say why it had happened. True, the heir to the throne had been murdered. But nobody knew him; we were seeing his picture for the first time. Our fear was like that experienced at the sight of a threatening flood which one cannot stop. There was no talk of "imperialist expansionist tendencies" or "protection of Austrian honor." One felt only the terrible approach of a mysterious and eerie storm. People ran around upset or full of false calm. Women cried, initially a few, then all of them, as the first reservists were called up. These soldiers in peasant dress got drunk before marching off, slept a last time with their girls, then packed their military bags and walked on foot to the town, swaying and singing, accompanied by mothers and wives, all of them wailing and weeping. Mothers clung to their sons, sons to their mothers. Newlyweds went with blank faces to the edge of the village. The inn was besieged. No farm boy could say where he was going or why. It was just "to war."

I arranged for my brother to move in with relatives. He stayed there till 1918, when he, too, enlisted. We went to the capital. Border skirmishes had already taken place. In the main square

I saw a Landsturm company just returning from a battle. Here, for the first time, I saw a people's enthusiasm for war. The soldiers were decorated with flowers. They walked with dignity, their leader on horseback, with saber drawn. They had been fighting in closed columns. The Russians had learned about protective bunkers during the war with Japan, but the Austrians had not. The cream of our active soldiers died in those first weeks of the war, fighting in closed columns, shot down by Russians in skirmish lines.

The wealthier people of the province fled to the center of the Empire. The estates of the region were left without stewards. A few days after the outbreak of war, thick columns of Russian infantry poured into central Austria along the various roads. One of these roads passed by our house, where I lived alone with an elderly housekeeper. I had stayed because I didn't want to abandon the business and also because I did not want to enter the unknown. There was also some romanticism involved. Before the Russians reached our village, I had played at war. I saddled my horse and rode out "to meet them." I was very angry with them. I would not have known how to explain why. In my pocket I carried a pistol. I was lucky not to run into a Cossack patrol; I would have fared badly. The first Cossacks were frightening. They looked warlike and brutal. But they did no harm and only asked where the Austrians had gone. The population stood on both sides of the road and stared. I had been told, to avoid plundering, to set up some barrels of schnapps at the side of the road. This had a great effect; but the wrong one. The officers found my house to their liking, decided to stay the night, and did their best to be very polite. The soldiers bivouacked in the large courtyard. Some of them helped themselves to honey from the beehives and were terribly stung—just like ordinary people. At the time, I was afraid they would shoot me because I had not warned them. Finally, an officer forbade the stealing of honey. But he demanded grain and promised to pay for it from a supply train which was to follow. I gave them the grain, but never saw any money. I remember my silent astonishment that these Russians could behave so humanly and do me no harm. Work on the farm proceeded, but on a somewhat reduced scale.

In the village there were some so-called Russophiles. They befriended the Russians and were afraid they would be hanged when the Austrians returned. In their eyes, I was not an exploiting landowner, but obviously an "Austrian." One evening, things really turned nasty. I was reading in my room. The gas lamp stood beside me. All of a sudden, a shot rang out simultaneously with the crash of a windowpane. I threw myself to the floor and crept into the adjoining room, which was dark. Later I was told that it had been Russophiles from the village who "hated the Austrian rulers." A disagreeable-looking village blacksmith was suspected. When the Austrians returned, he was denounced and later hanged. I felt badly about the whole incident, and I was in no way convinced that he had been the culprit.

People's imaginations ran wild; spies were suspected everywhere. The wish to see someone hanged and the fear of being hanged oneself drove people to do things which, though at that time they were deadly serious, today seem to me simply indications of a psychosis.

In the village, a Russian sergeant major stayed behind with some soldiers as an occupation force. He liked to have me give him money and some present or other. I was pleased to give him what he wanted and was even on very good terms with him. There was no fighting in our district. After a few weeks, the Russians retreated to the border and the Austrian cavalry pulled in. I rode happily to meet them and called out to the first patrol. It disappointed me that they looked tired and did not sit straight in their saddles as military representatives of Austria.*

In order to protect myself from attacks by Russophiles, I moved

---

*A similar thing happened some fifteen years later, when I first drove across the Soviet border and saw a Red Army man. I shook his hand warmly and enthusiastically, but he only looked at me in bewilderment and without understanding. It was this way with me for a long time in my life. Something was very earnestly propagandized and I would take it seriously. Then, time and again, I discovered that I had taken it more seriously than the propagandizer.

to a Ukrainian professor's house. Again the Russians marched in and stayed a long time. Then they left. But this time they took hostages with them—which, it was said, meant Siberia and eventual execution. They took me along, I suppose because of my "importance." It happened this way:

Early one winter morning, while I was still asleep, the Russian sergeant major came to the professor's house, accompanied by two men with fixed bayonets, and asked for me. The sergeant major said with regret in his voice that he had been ordered to take me to Russia as a hostage. Many others would be coming along. I tried to stall for time and asked if I could take my own horse sleigh. He said yes. To the steward, who had come rushing in, I whispered to collect as much money as possible in the village and to follow the hostage train as quickly as he could. I had very little cash, and everything depended on the willingness of friends to help me.

My sleigh was last in the train heading for the Russian border. Many furs were taken along, for it could reach 40 degrees below in those districts. I felt no fear, but was cool and calm as I always was in perilous situations. The sergeant major rode behind my sleigh. I had placed myself facing him. The coachman, a young peasant I was very fond of, was terribly upset and almost in tears. I winked at the sergeant several times. After a while, he understood. But I still had no money and there was nothing to be seen of the steward. About an hour outside the village, I saw a team approaching us at great speed. Hoping it would be the steward, I told the coachman to drive slower and fall a little behind. The sleigh came nearer. As it drew abreast of the sergeant, the steward handed him a packet of bank notes. Gradually, we fell farther behind, till it was safe to turn. The Russian sergeant seemed happy—not only because of the money—and rode away. I do not know what happened to the other Austrians. Later I heard that a neighbor had died in captivity.

We had to drive the sleigh over a high bridge across a stream. The coachman was nervous and so the horses shied continuously. Luckily he advised me to get out of the sleigh before the bridge, for the horses shied again just as he was crossing the bridge and both he and they fell into some two meters of water. Nothing terrible happened, and we arrived home pale from the scare, to be revived by several glasses of strong schnapps.

At this time I was in love with a schoolteacher. The Austrians marched in again and held the front at Zaleshchiki, an Austrian border town a two-hour wagon trip from us. The thunder of cannon could be heard. The Russians broke through again, and when the Austrians retreated, I decided not to stay, but to join up as a volunteer. I sent all the livestock, cows, oxen, and horses across the Prut with the steward. My wagon was loaded with the remaining sacks of feed, and when the whole caravan drove off, I stayed behind to see to last-minute affairs. The teacher with whom I was friendly was going to come along in my wagon. She, too, did not want to stay, even though she was Ukrainian. We were still eating when a youth burst in, crying out that the hill was black with Cossacks. I looked and saw that the kilo-meter-long hill across from my house was indeed swarming with riders. As we drove off, some of the village children threw stones at us.

The road from the border led through a long valley, into which we had just turned. Approximately in the middle of the valley, we saw to our left an Austrian lancer patrol, fleeing at a racing gallop across the valley, toward the opposite slope. Some of the lancers fell from their horses. Behind them appeared the Cos-sacks in extended order, firing at a gallop on the Austrians. My companion grew deathly pale. I told her to hide in the bottom of the wagon, and I did likewise. The coachman whipped the horses and we tore along until we were away from the dangerous encounter between the enemy patrols.

By the bridge over the Prut, I saw countless refugees, carts, and cattle of all sorts. At the same time, German cavalry, covered by the Austrians, rode off. On the other side of the river, we met our people who had been waiting for us. We resumed our journey. On the way, I sold the best draft horses to a division of the Austrian Army. The cattle and the rest of the horses remained with the steward in a large market town, also to be sold. I never saw either my homeland or my possessions again. Of a well-to-do past, nothing was left. I stayed with the teacher's mother for a few days, but it made little sense to remain there. The steward later sent some of the money to my military post.

I reported for military service half a year earlier than I was due to, legally, and was assigned to a division which built roads and simultaneously practiced with weapons. As a volunteer, I did not yet have the right to a commission, because I had not got my secondary-school diploma. But twelfth-grade pupils could get a *Notabitur*, or emergency diploma. You had to make up the courses of the final year and pass a somewhat leniently judged examination. My school friend Sabinski was in Suceava, a small town in southern Bukovina, with his father, who was working on the railway. I was given leave and took the examination there. In the late summer of 1915 I moved to the cadre unit of the 80th Infantry Regiment, in Hungary. My friend went into the 41st, and fell in his first battle. By this time, I was in officers' school. We were eighteen-year-old boys, as were some thousands in the Eastern Army. With six weeks of infantry training behind us, we were being instructed in extended and platoon company leadership. The schooling was strict and difficult. The worst were the young first lieutenants, who had come straight out of cadet school at the start of the war and had been promoted immediately. I got to know the chicanery of the drill regulations very well. At that time, we took everything for granted. We did not think about whether it made sense. The whole thing was merely a logical continuation of the school situation: the teachers of the officers' school replaced our high-school instructors. We had already had shooting lessons in the next-to-last class of high school. I had won a second prize at free shooting, the first in my class. I stress the fact that I undertook military schooling uncritically and without thought. I was even intent on doing my job well. From a militarist's point of view, I was "a competent, hardworking man." I returned to the regiment a full corporal. Most of the men were lance corporals. In the spring of 1916, I was given command of a platoon in an infantry battalion and moved off into the field.

I knew no socialists in the regiment, and there were none; at least, they did not make themselves noticeable. The one-year volunteers, as officer candidates, had close contact with the leaders of the regiment. We were strictly separated from the soldiers, inwardly as well. This was due primarily to the difference in uniform, which took center stage for the officers, commissioned and noncommissioned alike. Everything revolved around the stars and the yellow braid. We dreamed of becoming officers. Then we could carry a long saber instead of the bayonet. Even the sergeant major was envied for that. Whoever carried a saber had far more success with girls than anyone who carried a bayonet. Likewise, the machine gunner had more success than the infantryman, and the artilleryman or cavalryman far more than a company of infantrymen. In the cadre, there were brothels for officers and brothels for soldiers. The officers lived privately, as did the volunteers. They could eat by themselves. The troops lived in barracks and had to eat in the mess. One was not allowed to be seen together with a private on the street. The one-year volunteers who had failed their examination were no longer our equals. If an officer had a girl, no noncommissioned officer dared go near her, let alone a private soldier. The hierarchy was absolute, as was the separation between officers and men. The noncommissioned officers were strictly held to not yielding to the soldiers. Every method of enforcing discipline was allowed. I had about sixty men under my command. They were mostly men between thirty and forty years of age. Those in command were eighteen to twenty years old. The lieutenant who commanded the infantry company was twenty-two years old. We were strict, because that was the way to become an officer. We did not know why. Three-quarters of our strictness was vanity. Something had been made out of nothing, which was itself a nothing when faced with a higher rank. Insubordination on the part of a soldier was considered an insult to "honor"; honor was expressed by a star. If we did not greet a superior on the street, we were immediately "de-starred." The same applied to our subordinates. We believed firmly and honestly in the essential nature of dignity. The whole world appeared to depend on it.

And it did depend on it. Without the honor of the star and without the simple man's respect and longing for it, no war would have been possible, in spite of all the imperialistic motives. No one had the slightest notion of imperialist controversies.*
We were simply prepared from childhood for subjugation to the ideology of the war machine. There was nothing fundamentally new about war; it was simply the test of the strength of the old authority. People could withstand this test very well because they suddenly became something after having been nothing (especially the country-bred soldiers, who had for the first time been exposed to another world). The masses were dumbly obedient; in groups, they were vain and proud of serving in the army. Only a very few gave voice to their highly unpatriotic fear. In the course of the war, I came in contact with thousands of people, and in close contact with hundreds. But I do not recall one who had any understanding of the war or of its function.

In the spring of 1918, people began to feel the war was senseless. It was at the time of the Vienna–Neustadt munition workers strike. Sabotage was more a result of lethargy than of any coherent understanding.

We experienced this senselessness very gradually through a series of events which spoke a far clearer language. Like millions of others, from being a sort of patriot, I turned into a politically unaware saboteur.

When my battalion came to the front, we dug in, in positions about five hundred meters behind the most advanced trenches. We were in front of both the tunnels on the Gorizia–Monfalcone stretch, hence on the leftmost wing of the Italian front. At nightfall we marched in goose-step with picks and immediately set the stone drillers to work. From somewhere ahead of us, at regular intervals, came grenades and shrapnel. During the first

*And just as little notion of the structural anchoring of the state in the person.

night, everybody was afraid. Then we became accustomed to it and automatically dropped flat on the ground, just as we did when searchlights or rockets lit up the sky. Off and on, someone would cry out and have to be carried away. In time, this also became automatic, as in a well-run office. Soon it went unnoticed: *habituation and dulling.*

Then we were detached and moved into the trenches. I was assigned a dugout with room for twenty men. We were forty. The entrance to the dugout cleverly faced the "enemy." Every half minute, a small-caliber cannon from the chimney of a nearby factory shot a grenade exactly into the corner of the trench where the entrance lay. Within a few hours, we got used to it and did not leave the dugout until the next grenade had hit. But while we were getting acclimated, some of the men were wounded. War reporters and historians surpass themselves in describing details of the toilsomeness of fighting and dying. I, like most others, experienced the war as a machine, which, once set in motion, works senselessly according to its own rules. In the orders and in the drill regulations, it stated that during "rest pauses" every company had to post one or two sentries. Automatically, we posted two of them right in front of the entrance to the dugout. Duty is duty and service is service. One after the other, they were hit. Finally, I ordered the sentries to stand inside the dugout. During one of the following nights, a barrage began which lasted for six days and nights. It was the sixth Italian offensive. Between the dugout and the trench there were about eight paces of free terrain with no breastwork. The telephone connection between the dugout and the company command post was broken. Repairing it cost several men's lives. In descriptions of war, such events become heroic deeds. They are not heroic deeds; they are automatic actions, stupid deaths. Army orders stated that provisioning was to be in the trenches. But food did not reach us; one column after the other was broken up on the way. When the barrage let up, we finally had food in the trench. We took it into our mess kits. There was noise; a few grenades; a few dead. That is what a hero's death for the fatherland looks like. During night attacks, most of us shot blindly into the dark. If, during a battle, all soldiers were calmly to make use of their skill as sharpshooters, after a few days there would be no more armies. Mass death is only to be ascribed to the abundance of spent ammunition. Individual action, in which one kills knowingly, is the exception. This is considered the usual action of the purposeful warrior, but it is not true. When participants in the war report such actions, they are only giving in to their passion for glory. In the little film footage shot during the war, it is the lethargy and the automation of the attacking soldiers which is striking. One advances dumbly, throws oneself dumbly on the ground, shoots blindly.

Faced with fire which could not be returned, many prayed. Many cried out in a most unsoldierly manner for their mothers or just whimpered quietly to themselves. I remember a reserve company moving into one of the most advanced trenches. It is something I shall never forget. We were standing in the openings between sandbags. There were relatively few grenades. Times like this were known as "nothing new to report at the front." The company moved in, they were young peasant boys between eighteen and twenty years of age. Our sergeant major guided their entry march. Whenever a grenade burst, they would throw themselves to the ground and would not move. As they lay in heaps, blocking the way, the sergeant major, in despair, hit them on their backs with a stick. But they would not move and cried out to God and mother for help. A few days later a grenade tore off both this sergeant major's legs and he died.

If one had been in the trenches a long time and had experienced some real barrages, soldierliness was soon lost and the human side came to the fore. There was scarcely any difference between officers and men. We helped each other as best we could and spoke together of things which were not otherwise customary. One developed a gallows humor, protecting oneself from the thought of one's own death. One armored oneself. This humanization the German warmongers called "front experience." By using it to promote war enthusiasm, they reversed its meaning. Those into whose heads they were drumming the front experience were still in the phase of pride in uniform stars.

I became ill from a bad skin inflammation as a result of the damp and was sent to the rear.* Then, twice more, I went to the front. The second time was in April 1918 for the Isonzo offensive, fought with the help of German troops. About 400,000 Italians were taken prisoner. Daily their columns would march past our encampments. Most of them were happy to be prisoners. The officers hid this happiness beneath a shared façade of dignity. There was no trace of personal enmity.

We all experienced the impersonal character of the war, its machinelike progress. But no one understood the contradiction between this and the propaganda which painted the enemy on the other side of the barbed wire as the personal sworn enemy of each one of us. This influencing of our minds was accepted just as thoughtlessly and just as much a matter of course as the human, even friendly nature of the imprisoned "enemy" once we finally saw him firsthand.

The Italian prisoners brought their brothels with them: an older woman with four or five girls. Our people when on reserve were given "brothel leave." In Fiume and Trieste this business flowered in a ghastly way. The soldiers were lined up alphabetically to go to one girl. The Italian women were quartered in our camp. By day, some of the batmen and some of the men slept with them. The following night, the officers took them into their rooms. Three days later, a whole column marched back to the rear with gonorrhea. Among them, our captain. So much for morality.

One evening at about ten o'clock, our artillery opened up a murderous fire. It lasted a few hours, then we moved forward,

---

*In January 1913, I had had to interrupt my studies; psoriatic "plaques" had appeared on my elbows. My father took me to a well-known skin specialist, who prescribed a strong chrysarobin salve. This caused a severe dermatitis, and I lay for nine months in the Ehrmann Clinic in Vienna, where I was treated with X-rays. Afterwards, my skin was always very delicate, reacting to the slightest irritation.

second in line. The first line was a little ahead. Nobody knew quite where we were going or how. But we trotted along, past the Italian trenches. The bodies lay in rows from earlier attacks. We rested in an abandoned dugout. In front of the dugout were barbed-wire fences, hung with bodies. They made no impression.

I went back to the front for the third time as a lieutenant and company commander, this time into occupied upper Italy. We lay in reserve near Gemona [del Friuli]. Food was scarce and discipline had become loose.

We constantly had to parade. I was friendly with a first lieutenant, a lawyer, who was very clever and worldly. He told me that our professional future was lost. We had already been in the war for three years, torn out of civilian life; soldiers from habit. We could hardly imagine being able to earn our own living again. He suggested that we let ourselves be "activated" as officers. We would then remain with the army after the war; we were no longer good for anything else. We had inwardly lost faith that we would win the war. It kept on endlessly. You went to the front, then on leave, then to the cadre, then back to the front. This time we lived among the Italian people, ate with them, played with their children, had no feeling of being their enemies. We had our girlfriends among them who took care of us as though we were one of their own people. I lived with a young woman whose husband was on active duty with the Italian Army. She had a little child. We talked together a lot. She loved her husband. He had been gone two years. She did not know where he was. She supported herself and her child with great difficulty. They owned a piece of land which produced corn, and grapes for wine. Most of it lay fallow. The armies which had marched through had eaten everything.

Quite unconsciously, like everyone else, I relaxed discipline. If my company drifted far away during exercises, I would let them rest instead of making them throw hand grenades or climb over stone fences. One time the colonel surprised me. But I told him of the meager meals and the superabundance of orders. He said nothing more. As this sort of thing was also happening in other companies, the officers were called together and made to practice the handling of weapons for two hours at a time. We knew we were supposed to be maintaining discipline.

By this time, the Russian revolution had broken out. Russia was the first to have learned the lesson. We heard rumors, but there was little in the papers, and what there was was all wrong. The word Bolshevik reached us, but we did not attach any meaning to it. It was too far away and we continued to trot along as before. This as a commentary on the phrase about the "inflammatory effect" of revolutionary events on the soldiers of other countries. We were not held back by machine guns, but were inwardly laid waste, no longer capable of taking anything in. The Ukrainian and German soldiers of our regiment knew far less. In 1918, everything could have been smashed to bits. But we had our personal worries. For example, how to get hold of more meat for the men. The Italians butchered their cattle, illegally, at night. I took better care of my company by raiding the Italians by night and commandeering their illegally butchered oxen. At that time I was much beloved by the company soldiers. I got to know the men from a new angle; behind the dullness, the blind obedience, the boring obscene jokes, there was hidden not a "revolutionary class consciousness and hatred of the ruling class" but a deep human simplicity and straightforwardness. It never dared show itself in the open, but it crept forth when the girdle of authoritarian discipline was loosened. Then, very cautiously and slowly, it came to light. An older soldier was badly scolded by the sergeant major for some "negligence." I was given the report of the "crime." I made little of the matter. Thereupon, the soldier started crying. I was not far from it myself. These people had a deep feeling and understanding for a mind-set which was not warlike. They would not have grasped the words "Down with the imperialist war." But right here, in their highly unsoldierly humanity, lay the power which could have been mobilized against the "imperial war." Not one of us realized it, though the knowledge was germinating in us all. In those days I would not have been able to put my feelings into words. But we would have all breathed a sigh of relief if someone had found the words and spoken to us.

Soon a general disillusionment set in which manifested itself as indolence or in expressions of humanity. The militarist calls it "slackness" and "pacifism." It gripped the men as well as the reserve officers. Some active soldiers retained their military "cramp"; without it, their lives would no longer have had any meaning. We others wanted to learn new professions, or carry on with our old ones. It became obvious that to be warriors was not a practical justification for existence. We felt it, but did not know it. The machinery ran, kept in motion by the passivity of the masses and the brutality of a few career officers. Almost everything went wrong at a big maneuver which the division carried out in the vicinity of Udine, shortly before moving up to the advanced lines. According to the old standards, three-quarters of the troops would have deserved to be "strung up." But this was not possible now, and anyhow, "stringing up" had been abolished. So one muddled on. I had had enough of it. It was possible to get a three-month leave to study, and I handed in my request with some others and was furloughed. I went to Vienna and joined the law faculty. It was the end of August 1918. I was twenty-one years old and had lost four years of study.

But law was not for me. I undertook it because one could earn one's living more quickly here than elsewhere. There were three-month cram courses for the first state exam. I studied industriously, but without inner involvement. Two weeks before the examination, filled with hundreds of paragraphs of Roman and ecclesiastical law, I ran into an old school friend who was studying medicine. He reawakened my interest in natural science. I dropped jurisprudence, and transferred to the faculty of medicine. It was a good intuitive move; a few weeks later Austria fell, and with it, its administration of justice. I would have gone under, as I was without any material basis of existence. I lived two more months on my lieutenant's pay, then I was demobilized.

The collapse of the monarchy and the army was experienced

by most people without much excitement. The removal of the Emperor by the National Assembly was accomplished almost soundlessly, with only a few shots fired in the vicinity of the Parliament. To us, none of it mattered. We were looking for the way back into life.

THREE

Vienna
1918–1922

My medical studies at the University of Vienna lasted four years, instead of the usual six. Students who had fought in the war had the right to finish three semesters within two years, rather than spend a full year on each. This meant working harder, because the medical student who was a veteran had to be as much an expert in his field as the others. I graduated as a doctor of medicine in the summer of 1922. Those four years, crammed with experience, were to affect all the others to come. Unconsciously, they laid the foundation for my theory of sex-economy. I say unconsciously, because I was a completely innocent student, one of thousands, without any pretensions to a better life, satisfied with the hope of one day being able to practice a decent profession and make a decent living. I fought for material independence.

Breaking away from my family was concurrent with being able to support myself. Two of my father's brothers lived in Vienna. Though not rich they were materially so well off that my brother and I could easily have been taken care of financially. The remnants of our former property were unobtainable. After four years of war, nobody was able to bring any order into the legal confusion. Added to this, our native province had fallen to Rumania. A court case to salvage our farm property (the very existence of which was questionable) would have used up more money than it was worth. My renunciation was therefore without regret. My father's life insurance was completely devalued.

It is the great luck of life-insurance companies that they can legally pocket the premiums in good times, in order, equally legally, to avoid full payment of the insured sum in bad times. Here, a bad period—currency devaluation or something similar —comes to their aid at the right moment. Nobody reads the two hundred insurance regulations and clauses at the end of the contract. In this way, my brother and I were forced into beggary. An aunt who lived in America sent us a few dollars now and then. In addition, one of our two uncles, who liked us, would sometimes give us a hundred Austrian kronen, which had just been devalued.

At first, we occasionally ate with our relations. But family ties look different in practice: my uncles' wives gave their own children precedence. During the years of hunger, what we ate left less for them. It was embarrassing and embittering. One day an aunt served her children coffee; afterwards, she gave me a watered-down serving. I knew that she would never have given this to her own children. I left without a word, slammed the door behind me, and never saw those relations again. There was a student cafeteria which then was the only place I ate. But for two years we ate oatmeal with dried fruit day in and day out. On Sundays, we had two pieces of jam cake. Since the woman who served us liked me, I sometimes got a double helping. Bread and sugar were rationed, as were meat and other important foodstuffs. We received one-quarter, and later only one-eighth, of a loaf of bread per week. This I ate immediately, with yellow castor sugar sprinkled on it. We were starved and frozen. Poor people got no coal, so I studied in a small café, where an iron stove burned. I came to love that café. Early in the morning, at seven or half past, two hours before my first class, I studied, with great pleasure, physics, chemistry, and biology. I was to take the first half of the first oral examination for my medical degree by the end of December. I lived in an unheated furnished room with my brother and another student, who later became a psychoanalyst. I mention the fact that he sometimes received food from his mother because in those days it played a big role in my struggle with homesickness. I don't know how we survived those first months.

We sold for almost nothing some valuable pieces of clothing and some small pieces of furniture which we had managed to save. The regimental command issued our severance pay, but there was a muddle, and the demobilization office in Vienna paid it a second time. I did not clear up the mistake. I had given the state much more: four young, hopeful years. When you are hungry, wrong becomes right, and right wrong. I had no scruples. I borrowed the necessary textbooks from colleagues. I do not recall how I scraped together the payment for the first year of study and the cram course.

After I took the oral examination in physics, chemistry, and biology, my situation became easier. I started giving cram courses to colleagues and soon had a lot of students. I learned even more by teaching; it obliged me to explain what I had learned mechanically for the examination. In this way, I supported myself as best I could for about three years. Later I taught anatomy. I had passed the first set of medical oral examinations with the top grade in every subject.

The students organized themselves to cope better with the great misery of those first postwar years. They accomplished a lot. There was a German, a Jewish, and a nonnational students' union, the Vienna Medical Association. I belonged to the last. The war veterans had a special position at the university. They were usually from two to four years older than the regular students. They were experienced, grownup men, from whom the younger student generation differed in every respect, particularly in their relations with the female students. Soon there were many liaisons. Studying together was difficult, but it was done with passion. Aside from studying and cultivating relations with friends of both sexes, we did nothing. Like the majority, I experienced the great political events of those years from a one-sided viewpoint which I have never found described in any political textbook. Our teacher of anatomy was Professor Tandler, a famous anatomist and social hygienist. He was a strict but excellent teacher, and we learned anatomy with enthusiasm. We related to him as a teacher, but not as a socialist. We knew little of this movement, even though our lives, and the student organization, put us in the middle of the political ferment. Once, in the fall of 1918, Professor Tandler asked us to help with the demobilization of the homecoming soldiers. Not one of us suspected that here a piece of Social Democratic disarmament policy was being played out with regard to our own people.

Everybody was totally taken up with his own studies and with keeping alive as best he could. We studied from early morning till late at night, in order to master the mass of material. We ate quickly in the student cafeteria after standing in line for one or two hours with our notebooks held in front of our noses. Many kept up with their studies with great difficulty, and some not at all.

During the years leading up to my graduation, I experienced everything in confusion, without inner coherence: socialism, the Viennese intellectual bourgeoisie, psychoanalysis, and my unhealthy fixation on my early experiences.

I was regarded as a promising doctor, especially by my relatives. Prior to my breaking with them, they tried to "marry me to someone rich." In this way, I was to be relieved of my poverty, which was very great. It was not easy to say no. I lived over a year in abstinence, with occasional masturbation, and longed for a woman. But I wanted to be free and was afraid of tying myself down. I was engaged for a short time to a pretty girl, but she didn't want to sleep with me, and she could not talk sensibly either. I dropped her. After thinking it over, I turned down two or three offers to sell myself to a rich girl.

Female colleagues would take me to medical get-togethers and private gatherings. We were all very clever and well educated, and even indulged in a bit of spiritualism, "for fun." The girls liked me as a dancing partner because I danced well. They flirted a lot, and hid their sensuality behind clever talk or intellectual dignity. They could get very excited while dancing, but no expression gave it away. They were all afraid of a serious relationship, just as they were of the open admission of what they unconsciously felt. I saw through their behavior and spoke with them about these things.

Most of these girls lived in warm, apparently well-adjusted families. This bothered me, for I was jealous; I was freezing and nobody took care of me. It annoyed me that they had to be home on the most beautiful Sundays at one or two in the afternoon, since their mothers would otherwise be "hurt." I was invited out often. The mothers were usually very fretful and neurotic, unhealthily attached to their children, devastated without them. Some of the girls were aware of this. Yet they were considerate. In so being, many of them wore themselves out and regretted it later, too late. The parents were friendly and kindhearted, but they watched over their daughters' chastity, threatening to break down if their children were to misbehave while unmarried. The girls suffered from the necessary self-control, consciously or unconsciously, but they didn't want to "grieve" their parents. I could never understand how their daughters' fulfilled love could seriously harm the parents. The boyfriend of a female colleague was a medical student. They were often together and wanted to get married. Before it came to that, two years had passed. Until then, they had never embraced one another. I had absolutely no understanding of that kind of behavior, which at the time was highly regarded and praised. It seemed to me pathological. These girls sensed my attitude and it pleased them. But they never overstepped certain boundaries, even the twenty- and twenty-four year-olds.

There were others who did exactly the opposite. They came from the same proper, upper-class homes, but they slept with everybody who chanced their way. I never had any serious friendship with these girls, or if I did, it was when they became healthier. In my diary I called the chaste ones, who were afraid of falling, "whores"; the others were unhappy creatures, whose sickness I later, as a psychoanalyst, had many opportunities to study. Chastity was just as serious an illness, but I only understood its meaning much later.

The atmosphere in the girls' homes and their sexual restraint made me neurotic. When my mind was clear, I felt myself an "outsider." I longed for a home with parents and at the same time feared it. But I knew that I had to make myself free inwardly. Freeing myself from this longing for a home took some years. But it entailed no ideology which I wanted to impose on others; I was neither for nor against the family, sensed nothing of its function, and felt only the morbidity of my own longing for a home and the restriction imposed by it on my friends.

I read a great deal over and above my studies, and was often disturbed by manifestations of abstinence. I had no idea that the wild enthusiasms which overcame me at times, the overexcitement of my senses, and a certain restlessness, were the result of a lack of sexual gratification. In 1919 I came to know Weininger's *Sex and Character*. This book, written by an unfortunate but clever philosopher, was read by all intellectuals and raved over. I read Schopenhauer's *Aphorisms* and tried Kant. I lacked all prerequisites for the understanding of *A Critique of Pure Reason*. There were colleagues who spoke a lot about it, and I was embarrassed that I did not understand it. Later I knew that they did not understand it either and had only been letting off clever hot air. Being clever was a special sport of the bourgeois elite, especially of the Jewish youth. Cleverness for its own sake, to be able to talk wittily, to develop ideas, and to philosophize about the thoughts of others were some of the essential attributes of a person who thought something of himself. I admit that I could not keep up with this, although I was not stupid. Much was obscure to me, and some things even seemed wrong. They contradicted my sense of what the world was about. "The world as will and representation" was a wonderful idea, it impressed me very much, but, but . . . I knew nothing about it and even less what to do with it. Though inwardly I felt I was correct, I felt inferior. My life was constantly affected by this contradiction. I stayed in the background at first and only came forward slowly. But when I had worked out a position, that position triumphed, I emphasize, without my having made a plan. For more than a decade, I defended views against which my inner feeling warned me, but to which I had no alternative to offer. In short, I have never in my life indulged in fantasies of being a genius or of becoming one.

During my student years I came up against the best minds of Vienna. And it always happened that I followed a way alien to me, until the admonitions of my inner resistance became too strong and I broke away. On the basis of such behavior, I was later accused of being unreliable. Only today do I know that, intuitively, I was on the right track. By getting to know everything exactly and at the same time remaining self-determined, I learned to exercise *productive* criticism.

Not that I wanted to become an "objectively correct critic." On the contrary, I gave myself up to impressions quite uncritically. Nor was this done to make myself an especially good student. Each subject with which I became involved consumed me completely. This caused me a lot of suffering, but I would not want to have missed it. It was my greatest strength.

*   *   *

Feb. 25, 1919

9 a.m. Convention of the organization of Jewish university graduates of Vienna. Were we going to have to listen to the same old platitudes? Perhaps from a different slant? But no, something new appeared on the horizon, something I had never noticed before in Jewish sentiments of any sort: not the all too familiar wailing, not the tirades against everything non-Jewish (which, because of my contrary convictions, have caused the dilemma in which I find myself today), but a new trend, born of strictly socialistic ideals—not the old "race against race" but a new, encouraging "people for people" attitude. Many speakers, lots of talk, not very meaningful, the usual on such occasions. But there was one among them, a Dr. Bergmann from Prague. What

a wealth of intellectual content he presented! He expressed my innermost feelings—I anticipated every word, could almost physically feel the thoughts surfacing from my own subconscious. Much that had been lying dormant within me was aroused, I saw clearly on so many issues—and hundreds of others must have seen clearly as well. There was no hatred for everything non-Jewish, but a meaningful receptiveness to others; no controversy over Jewish versus Hebrew, over blue-and-white versus red-and-green,* but expansiveness in all directions, renewing itself in ever-widening circles. Down came the impenetrable barriers, and then—the word came to me—international cosmopolitanism in the broadest sense! I confess that, for the first time since hearing or experiencing similar speeches, something arose within me—an explanation! This was the reason why I hated—yes, hated—all those who endeavored to help the Jews attain happiness—not along with other human beings, but over their dead bodies; not with the consent of others, but against their will! Not "we are all together," but just "*we*"! And finally I was listening to a man who is both a Jew and a human being simultaneously, not a chauvinist! We shall see what kind of fruit his efforts will bear.

A female colleague with whom I had dissected the upper portion of a cadaver was seated in front of me. Seems to have come for the sole purpose of showing off her blue silk outfit. She was ecstatic at the opening lines of some hackneyed speaker.

Was invited for tea at 5 p.m. at the apartment of a female fellow student named Neumann. The lady of the house was very charming, first impression excellent, then joined several of the other guests in Neumann's room. Very pretty, good taste, more like a schoolgirl's room than a university student's. A trace of envy (I wish I did not have to put it into writing). The conversation had already turned to banalities. I remained silent, as usual, although I should have liked to speak up. Why? Grete†

*Colors symbolic of various organizations. [Trans.]
*Grete Lehner and (on the following page) Eduard Bibring—medical students who were later married and became psychoanalysts. [Eds.]

· 78 ·

arrived, smooth and sleek as ever. I greeted her and at the same
moment I recalled her *"Guten Tag, Kollege!"* from the Saturday
before last. Oh, these conventions which muzzle you at the very
moment you have so much to say you could burst! Bibring and
Singer arrived—Bibring in a frock coat which was too wide in
the front. But I was glad he came anyway, I enjoy watching him
so much! Then refreshments were served. There was an error in
the seating plan and I found myself between Grete and Neumann's brother. Just fine as far as I was concerned. I do not
enjoy *entertaining* ladies. The conversation couldn't seem to get
off the ground. Toward the end, it was somewhat more lively.
Groups formed—had a highly interesting discussion with Neumann's younger brother (a law student) on the subject of Jews
and the question of socialism. We are fairly well in agreement.
Danced at first with Miss Neumann and then with Grete. Why
do I enjoy dancing with her the most? Perhaps because she is
all woman then and not ... but what? I don't really know. I
prefer to view her as a woman rather than as a grave "acade-
mician." She's only charming when she's being naïve. After in-
dulging, unsuccessfully, in a little spiritualism, we all left. Felt
quite satisfied. The milieu, the lady of the house, and the brother
were extremely likable. While riding home, I thought with annoyance of the chemistry grind in the weeks ahead.

Feb. 27

Had a chance to talk with Grete alone and allude to several
matters. I do care very much about my friendship with this
intelligent girl, but before I proceed to deepen it, I must probe
her apparently complicated emotional life— which may exist only
to a very small degree or, what seems more likely to me, be
largely obscured by a substantial intellect.

My brother arrived from Bukovina. What a magnificent fellow! I wish him better luck than he has had until now! I feasted
my eyes on him—on his intelligent expression and the esprit of
that eighteen-and-a-half-year-old.

Tomorrow morning at eleven o'clock I have been asked "to

call" at Krugerstrasse 17, District I.* More humiliation. Oh, this dependency, having to "grovel," and how the philanthropists seem to enjoy it!

March 1

Today Fenichel† completed his lecture on "clitoral sexuality." Like all pupils of Freud, he sees latent sexuality in everything and everywhere. Even if it does hold true in the majority of cases, I do not agree with him completely.‡ Perhaps morality speaks against it, but my own experiences, my observations of myself and others, have led me to the conviction that sexuality is the core around which all social life, as well as the inner spiritual life of the individual, revolves—whether the relationship to that core be direct or indirect. Now this appears to contradict what I just said. We are all aware, however, that something is active within us, be it morality or aesthetics, which holds us back from believing this. We tend to deceive ourselves by trying to appear better in our own eyes. If one remains generally aware, in larger and smaller social circles, at all levels, and even in the academic community, one can easily satisfy oneself as to the probability of this theory. I do not make such claims under the influence of Freud's writings or today's lecture—*and as proof I offer the fact that I was already conscious of these things long before I began to study this science.* For example, I recall that during my childhood, conscious sexuality was awakened within me at the age of four through contact with the maids, i.e., their caring for me when my mother had to be away for several months due to illness. *I imagined sexuality in every glance, gesture, and especially in everything that seemed at all suspicious to me.* I personally have a strong sexual and

*Presumably, the address of Reich's uncle. [Eds.]
†Otto Fenichel—a medical student who, in January 1919, had organized a students' seminar in sexology at the university. He later became a psychoanalyst. [Eds.]
‡[Added in 1937] In these first lectures that I heard, the sexual had something bizarre and strange about it.

erotic disposition, although these elements have continually varied in their mode of expression from the first time I had sexual
intercourse (at age twelve) to the present day. My sexuality was
on the increase until I reached the age of twenty, when it attained
its peak, while my eroticism (in the sense Weininger and Krafft-
Ebing use that word) remained fairly latent until that time and
only then began to grow. Nowadays, it frequently happens that
*a woman excites me to the extreme in an erotic sense, without
my entertaining thoughts of coitus.* In such cases, however, I do
often catch myself undressing the woman with my eyes. Am I
to attribute this to sexuality or eroticism?*

March 2

3 p.m. Sitting in my room wearing gloves and fur coat, studying chemistry—no, I am forcing formulas into my brain, which
is resisting, refusing to assimilate them. The window is wide
open, the sunshine outside is enticing, but I enjoy playing the
role of a person with willpower. No street noise reaches my
room overlooking the courtyard. All I hear is the ticking of
my clock. I am tired, and as I lean against the window, I feel my
chest expanding with a wish. I wish . . . yes, but what do I wish?
On the floor below, someone was playing "Träumerei," then
came Schubert's "Schlaf ruhig, sei ruhig, mein Kind"—songs
which always fill me with nostalgia. I try to penetrate the wall
around the courtyard with my eyes; how beautiful the view from
here (the fifth floor) would be—directly out to the Kahlenberg
and the Kobenzl. At the same time I associate this with my
experiences last summer in Neuwaldegg when I did myself so
much harm—without being able to help it! In my blind search
for the happiness of having someone, just one person fully and
completely, I made the mistake of grasping recklessly and was
then forced, after only a few weeks, to break the self-imposed
chains. She was pretty and good, but lacked idealism, viewed
everything prosaically, constantly talking of being married, hav-

*[Added in 1920] How naïve!

ing children, making soup, and the like. I couldn't keep up with it! I want to live, but in a different way than you demand of me! Life, life, I scream for it, crave it, don't want to vegetate, grovel, surrender my personal dignity for two hundred kronen, stand outside the door for hours on end for a hundred kronen, just because there is a dragon in the house who dared to insult my mother and to whom I gave a suitable reply!* I don't want much! *But I don't want to go through school in order to prescribe ten aspirins a day, nor do I want to be compelled to go through school.* Don't rush me, don't rub my nose in your generosity every hour of every day, let me be a human being, don't suppress every emotion in me, every impulse which might make a better person of me. It is your fault that I shall never be capable of happiness, that I repress everything within me, that I am full of inner unrest and turmoil! How beautiful, how absolutely beautiful it could be! I look up at the sunny blue skies of springtime and something within is set in motion, calls out for fulfillment, something which could develop and bear beautiful fruit! And yet there is this *murderous pressure*, it weighs upon me, oppresses everything which is not useful for mere survival. *And the fact that there is no end in sight, that I know I might still be myself at a time when everything else within me will have died—that is the bitterest insight of all!*

March 3

Was enormously distracted today, couldn't keep my thoughts on my studies, or on any other subject. Was due to visit my uncle again at four o'clock, and my foreboding of what would take place at that time may well have been responsible for my condition. Naturally, once again I had no opportunity to speak to him. As Robert informs me (he is so much more practical than I and had already spoken with Uncle on the day he arrived), our uncle has agreed to lend "support," but only "*when he feels*

---

*An apparent reference to the conflict between Reich and his uncle and aunt. [Eds.]

like it." What prospects! I feel like a person who tried to sit between two chairs and landed on the floor. I want to visit Winia, to seek comfort and encouragement from a creature who is unhappy herself and deserves a better lot. At this very moment a name occurs to me: it is B. and I am ashamed of myself. And strangely, the first advice Winia gave me after I described my situation was to *get engaged, and to a wealthy girl*! (a woman's logic, definitely). But to whom?—B. again, and I am ashamed a second time. Although I had grown quite close to the girl, such a thought never even entered my mind, and now, suddenly, the thought presented itself twice. I was interested in B., in that sixteen-year-old girl who had emerged from a small town steeped in all its drawbacks and then, over the course of two years, had developed so magnificently in an intellectual sense. The traits which must have attracted me were her naturalness and the unaffected way she reacted to everything and everyone. After she left Vienna and I went into the service, we carried on a lively correspondence. Her straightforward, unartificial way of exchanging thoughts revealed many an aspect of her personality and her emotional life which she might never have disclosed to me consciously. It was then that the thought first occurred to me—quietly, with due consideration, not impetuously as might have been more in keeping with my age. And just this quietness was the reason why I was unable to understand the nature of my interest in the girl. Was it merely a passing interest, or was it more, perhaps the beginning of a serious attraction, of what could definitely be called love, as had befallen me once before and come to such an inglorious end? Robert spent three days there, raves about B., and assures me that she made the liveliest of inquiries about me. *May nothing serious come of this!* It could mean great unhappiness for her, she deserves something better, an inwardly firmer person. Winia's advice could easily be acted on, B.'s parents would have no objections either, but no, that would never do, *I would rob myself of my last bit of spine.* It would mean having my wife "keep" me (the very sound of it!). It could never form the basis for happiness as I picture it! The question of how else I am going to work my way out of the situation this year (not to mention next year) remains unanswered. *I am simply not the practical person my brother is.* To my great disadvantage, I have been imbued with much more idealism than is practicable. I strive for clearer vision and suffer the bitterest disappointments because of this.

March 8

Today I succeeded for the first time in reaping the benefits of studying Freud's theories by interpreting two dreams (one of them my own), and believe I arrived at a fairly plausible result. I plan to put it all down in writing, to occupy myself more with the interpretation of dreams, and to approach the practice of psychoanalysis via this method.

Spoke with my colleague Grete. I had told her of my argument with Arthur Pines over the importance of sexuality in the emotional and social life of women; also informed her of the fact that I could not agree with Weininger completely because I had her in mind as a case in point. I then came upon something which strikes me as highly interesting: she immediately remarked that she had frequently been made an example in such cases and asked me to describe the situation in detail. Today I did so, and I encountered a self-confidence in this girl which I would ordinarily have considered extreme conceit or self-complacence, although it actually was only to a small degree unjustified. The significance of this self-confidence in her life, and the extent to which it helps or hinders her, will be the object of my further observation of her. Wanted to start right in and hear her comments on self-confidence, but regrettably, I was disturbed by another colleague who joined us.

At four o'clock in the afternoon, on the way to a party given by the Jewish physicians, we were talking about marriage when I broached the subject of self-confidence—that factor whose absence seems to play such a large role in my own emotional life. Naturally, she realized immediately that I wanted to hear her opinion on her own self-confidence and told me exactly what

Reich's mother, Cäcilie Roniger-Reich, 1908

Reich's father, Leon Reich. On his copy of this photograph, Reich wrote of his father: "His ideal was the German Kaiser"

Reich's uncle, Arnold Reich. Leon Reich had hoped his son would
follow in Arnold Reich's footsteps and become a jurist

Wilhelm Reich at age three, 1900

Hunting party in Bukovina, 1912. Leon Reich second from left, Reich holding gun at his father's side, Robert Reich seated right foreground

Back from Officer's School as lieutenant, 1916

Scenes from the Great War, with Reich's own captions

Ready for combat

1916
Training in
Trench warfare

Dancing before Dying

Lia Laszky Swarowski, 1920

Annie and Wilhelm Reich

I expected to hear. Not only that she knew of the strength within her, of her self-confidence, but that she also was aware that this trait was disturbing in her relationships with certain people. And whoever couldn't handle it would simply have to do without her. She was also convinced that self-confidence helps more than it hinders. How true! *Yes, but what is self-confidence? Awareness of one's own value, which can only be relative, or the certainty of an inner strength, of the ability to achieve.* But here a question arises: does the awareness of this strength alone suffice to firmly establish self-confidence? *Is it not the work one actually accomplishes that gives one the objective right to be self-confident?* But then again, isn't accomplishment fundamental for subjective worth? Naturally, I do not mean worth in the eyes of others, for this can vary according to the individual who makes the judgment. If, however, self-confidence is based only on the consciousness of an inner strength, then I can't agree (with Bibring) that a person has the right to be self-confident who, although he does indeed possess the inner strength to achieve, has accomplished nothing- -due to some outside influence or his own inability. The meaning of the term "accomplishment" still remains debatable. My interpretation of the word would be, roughly, that man assimilates the printed word and intellectual knowledge, as well as impressions from without, and if he observes himself, through his own reactions to these impressions, he then processes, sorts, and employs these things for the improvement of his own judgment and objectivity, for accomplishments in his environment and in the other "fine arts" of life. When he has reached a certain degree of fulfillment in his work, he then begins to apply the material he has processed. This "reproduction" can partially suffuse his own ego and in part flow back into his environment after it has been enriched and modified by the ego's coloration.

And now to return to my friend Grete. She possesses not only the ability to achieve, she already *has* achieved; namely, she has assimilated knowledge within herself and trained herself to think in a way which is lacking in a major portion of our so-called intelligentsia. She is even on the road to applying her knowledge; she is not engulfed by it but stands above it. Therefore, her self-confidence is justified. I possess no self-confidence! And why? It is precisely this deficiency which has made me the person I am today, a brooder, pessimist and idealist simultaneously, equally as unhappy when I'm alone as when I'm in company, perpetually discontented, caviling at everything, although most of all at myself. *I have within me the strength and ability to achieve, I have assimilated great amounts of the printed word and intellectual knowledge, but all this lies within, not outside me—I am sitting in the midst of it, not above it*; it's as if I were in a crowd and could only see the people immediately surrounding me. I feel that I am not incorrect in claiming that it is this very situation which prevents any self-confidence from arising within me. For my own comfort, I must also admit that I have been active in the "reproductive" sense as well; I can tell myself that I contributed greatly to B.'s intellectual development, although only during periods when I did not consciously intend to do so. For this, too, is one of my peculiarities and constitutes a problem in my self-examination; namely, that I always fail when I make a conscious effort to be reproductive. *Everything is impulsive and spontaneous, never planned.* The "sitting in the midst" of the knowledge I possess today is certainly due to the lack of a systematic assimilation process—and to the fact that I was never able to find anyone to guide me. A not insignificant role was played by my unfortunate family situation, the four-year state of intellectual death,* and finally the disappointments which would not allow me to vent any emotions but rather constrained me to suppress whatever emerged.

March 15

Grete had invited me to go to a private dance scheduled for yesterday. I had said neither yes nor no but had firmly decided against going. All week long, I avoided meeting her, in the hope

*World War I. [Eds.]

that she would forget to mention it again. But, much to my chagrin and secret delight, she located me in the chemistry department yesterday (or had she only come in by chance with Bibring?), and I promised to come along. It was all very nice, I felt in excellent spirits and also discovered many new things about her. Impulsive, as I always am, I told her of my two "loves." What understanding I was shown in the second case especially! One of her comments: "Don't you think that my heart could also race someday?" Oh, yes, I certainly do! And how she would be able to love! Another one of her remarks (in response to my description of the ideal woman): "And have you ever found a woman like that?" I promptly replied: "No!" But how greatly she resembles my ideal woman, not so much physically as intellectually (and in this respect she even exceeds my ideal)! Yes, I was stupid enough to confess without further ado that if I should encounter that ideal I myself would probably be found wanting. I think this mania of mine—namely, lowering myself in her eyes—is developing into masochism. One more incident, I no longer remember how it came about: I kissed her hand, she held it out to me.

How uncomplicated and natural she was that evening! When she acts that way, I feel at ease in her company. And how pleasant she was in that room where we lingered in conversation with Dr. Stein. Yes, G. is a rare find! (What I have written above throws an unfavorable light on my feelings in view of the lies I tell myself.)

March 30
Grete got tickets for a performance of *Hölderlin* in the Kammerspiele. The play was poor, an unsuccessful attempt to portray the life of a poet in dramatic scenes.

Afterwards Bibring, Robi, and I went to the student cafeteria and were in fine spirits, which suddenly changed completely once we were home. Robi started to talk about our financial situation and remarked that if all our talks with Uncle Arnold came to naught, he intended to sell newspapers on Kärntnerstrasse and whenever Uncle Arnold passed by he would call out, *"Küss' die Hand, Onkel!"** We are in sad shape, nothing but uncertainty in the near future—the sole reason being that our uncle and legal guardian did not see to it that the insurance money was collected on time. Now he listens to our complaints with a shrug of his shoulders and his fists clenched in his pockets. I feel I will soon be confronted with the choice of "bend or break."

April 4

Called on Uncle Arnold today. The conversation yielded very little. His help consisted in advising me to "sell everything" so that I don't have to "go begging." All right, but what shall I sell? Robi and I could only subsist for two months at the most on the proceeds from the few remaining odds and ends of a better, more opulent era—and then what? Back to begging! The information I received at the insurance company was actually not very comforting, either. Claims from three sides on those few miserable kronen, and no possibility of even taking action to collect. Robi has enlisted in the German Army, Eastern Division.

April 5

Spent the afternoon, as I do every Saturday, in the Café Stadttheater. Once again, Grete was friendly. I was in a fairly good mood myself and we had a magnificent time. Also spent half an hour with N. in an adjoining room. Either I understand that woman too well or not at all. She shows an obvious interest in me, is annoyed that I don't want to go to the masked ball, thinks I only want to be coaxed—and five minutes later she tells me, half unwittingly and partially at my prodding, that she is in the midst of a love affair and that this time it's serious. She bores me as a social companion and yet this singular type of woman who longs to surrender herself and only waits to be taken interests me enormously. Sheer eroticism, sheer sensuality! She

---

*"I kiss your hand," an extremely respectful Viennese greeting. Highly ironic in this context. [Trans.]

sickens me. What a contrast, the intellectual, deeply spiritual girl in the other room (incidentally, also not without blemish), and this girl, whose every fiber vibrates with sexuality. I soon left her and returned to my own table. My good mood had vanished. We all broke up and I said goodbye to Grete and Bibring (although we were going in the same direction and could have walked together for ten minutes), was almost rude to the Neumann girl, who was walking to Mariahilferstrasse with Singer. Once again, I am in that inexplicable mood which disquiets me for days. There must be something pathological behind this. This self-torture is not natural. The reason for it lies either in my great vanity—or in a trauma stemming from that one horrible experience in my life! Or is it my ailment,* this ailment which causes me a thousand torments every hour and yet is no ailment at all. I fear that I am beginning to lose myself and will never find myself again!

April 9

Today I thoroughly sorted out all the articles full of memories of times so glorious that we are only now able to grasp the unpardonable casualness with which we took them for granted: Mother's embroideries and handiwork, which call to mind in detail every evening, every hour she worked on them; tablecloths, towels, and the like, pieces from a beautiful past which will have to serve the purpose of enabling us to exist miserably for one or two months. There will have to be haggling over things of immeasurable value to me; parts of a period of my life, with all the memories and nostalgia attached to them, will have to pass into the hands of strangers. And why? Because of the hard-heartedness and forever unforgivable negligence of a person who is both my father's brother and our guardian. I begged him not to leave us in the lurch, to lend us some money against a sum he is sure to collect. His answer: a shrug of the shoulders—"All I can do for you is offer my regrets." If these

*Reich is referring to his psoriasis. [Eds.]

comments should ever be read by an outsider, that person would certainly be completely amazed at this great display of senti-mentality, which must appear utterly nonsensical and inappro-priate in the light of mankind's present struggle over entire worlds, over universal revolutionary principles, where every individual is supposedly morally obligated to show concern for everything but himself. But here one might raise the question (although only a competent person should do so) of whether man does not carry the greatest wealth of ideas within his own ego, within his ex-periences and the memories of his childhood, of his *becoming* in general—but for that a soul is required! For people who merely flaunt the soul for the sake of impressing others, piety would be a better term. Many of them—yes, most—imagine themselves to be living solely for humanity. Twenty-four hours after my father's burial, I spent the night in a local café with women and music; five days after the death of my mother, Papa, Robi, and I sat in a nightclub crying over our champagne. Can anyone imagine such a thing? Even now, I have difficulty ex-plaining the reasons for my behavior! Neither after the death of my mother nor after that of my father did I cry as much as is "customary." I don't believe I even observed a year of mourning in my dress or in abstaining from entertainment—after all, why should I? The gentle pain within will remind me of the deceased for the rest of my life, and the *conscious* love for them which awoke, in me and in all the others, only after their death will never vanish. My question is, what purpose does mourning serve? Is it an exhibition to the outside world of the urgency of one's feelings? Not mourning, no, but that certain cringing of the heart which spreads to the brain and prevents you from swallowing, a feeling which arises when least expected, that is my grief, my pain—never noisy, but like a wave which swells within and ebbs back into itself.

April 28

Three weeks have passed, full of stagnation, idleness, and useless fantasies which were nevertheless beautiful (or perhaps all the more beautiful because of this). Dabbled here and there, read and studied a bit, didn't even suffer from depression as badly as before. The present erotic tension dominating me is noteworthy. It increases from day to day, and only disgust and fear of infection have prevented me from releasing it before now.

Ten days ago I met a young woman at Winia's. She is the wife of a merchant who is presently out of town and is supposedly a millionaire. In keeping with my feelings toward such people, I acted with utter reserve. I felt justified in assuming that the outlook of the monied aristocracy and that of the educated, and above all academic, world could never converge—their goals and *Weltanschauungen* rest on entirely different premises. By sheer coincidence (to this day, I do not know how it came about), a conversation developed on Zionism, on philosophy, and finally on social sexuality. In this last discussion, I soon quite unintentionally took the lead. The understanding and open-mindedness I encountered in the woman were a complete and pleasant surprise, and once again I came to the conclusion that one should never classify people according to "objective," generally accepted categories. She displayed an uncommon interest in my presentation of the gradually developing modern perspectives on the treatment of sexual issues, child education, etc. She had read Weininger and admits not having understood him completely. I offered to read several chapters with her. Furthermore, I am acquainting her with the theories of Freud and Jung, and we are presently reading a few chapters of *Freuds Neurosenlehre* together. The hours I spend there give me genuine pleasure and offer perfect intellectual refreshment.

At present I am giving a great deal of thought to the frequency and intensity of the daydreams which have been victimizing me recently, and to the significance I attach to them. They are usually similar in content and tend to satisfy unfulfilled longings. The desire for inner contentment, equilibrium, and rewarding work predominates. My abnormal ambition plays no slight part in this. Additionally, my longing for a woman emerges quite often. The one I envision is always the same; usually she has rich intellectual gifts. Despite the fact that these daydreams are always pleasurable, I do fear very much the distracting influence they have on my studies.

Dear Miss Lehner,

It will certainly surprise you that I have chosen this means of confrontation or inquiry when daily I have the opportunity to speak with you in person. I believe, however, that you will also agree, after due consideration, that many issues can be discussed better and less heatedly in writing than would be possible orally—due to facial expressions, searching for words, etc. But I am completely aware of exposing myself to one danger; namely, that of sounding ridiculous. This, in turn, is contingent on the frame of mind and mood in which a letter of such content is received. I therefore request that you take the trouble to read this note twice, with an interval between readings, before arriving at an opinion and giving an answer.

And now to the main issue: I feel that I am not mistaken in observing that our relationship—which was pleasant in the past, although never entirely free of all conventions—has of late, i.e., for approximately six weeks, been slackening. This was manifest in several events which were quite insignificant in themselves but nevertheless were embarrassing to me.

I fully realize that I am not completely blameless. It would be simple for me to explain the part I played in the discord, but for the moment I will bypass this. Later perhaps I shall find an opportunity to clarify. And now to cite two examples. Please do not think I am a petty person, I feel capable of differentiating between weighty and irrelevant matters. Several weeks ago, you took Singer and Bibring to the theater, or you arranged for or bought the tickets. I only discovered this by chance in the evening, before Bibring left. I could also see that it embarrassed him when I inquired where he was going.

It is possible that you had only a limited number of tickets at the time. But there might also have been many other reasons. I was quite shocked at the moment and, frankly speaking, I con-

sidered asking for an explanation the very next day, for I cannot bear secretiveness. At present, I can no longer say how it came about that I did not ask, but certainly cowardice played no insignificant role.

And now to the second reason for this letter, a letter which has begged to be written for a long time. Yesterday you, or actually your sister, told me of your outing, and once again you did not ask me to come along. Now I am on uncertain ground, for you will surely reply that I could have come along without having been invited and needn't have observed the rules of etiquette so precisely. You would be correct in this if such polite pretexts had not been employed lately. To clarify matters still further: even if I had been invited, I would have participated neither in today's outing nor would I have gone to the theater with you. The reasons for this lie in an entirely different area which has nothing to do with you or with our relationship.

I have come to know and respect you, Miss Lehner. Therefore, I do not wish to assume that my financial misfortune, and the resulting inability always to participate in everything, has caused this misunderstanding. You, Bibring, and Singer are certainly not overburdened with riches, but you are still more or less without material worries. I live from one day to the next and have been forced to go into debt for six months, to accept charity in order to struggle through. In my opinion, this is sufficient cause to make me a sullen, irritable, and frequently unpleasant fellow. Recently, I have withdrawn somewhat in order not to disturb anyone. If this makes me appear arrogant or ill-natured, it cannot be helped, for I do not like to bother others with my complaints. I bear this misfortune as well as I am able, after a pampered childhood—without annoying others. You may have some vague idea, but by no means can you fully judge what it means to be completely alone, to have no one with whom to share one's head-splitting thoughts, to be at odds with everyone, yes, even with oneself, and as a result of the entire situation, helplessly to observe an increasing necessity to exclude oneself. In anticipation of the present situation, I asked you once in the café not to pass judgment without knowing the facts. I now fear that matters have developed as I imagined they would. But since I do not wish to remain in the dark any longer—under any circumstances, and for the very reason that I value you so highly—I request that your reply be candid and frank. If I placed you on the same level as my other colleagues, I would not give the matter a second thought. But in my relationship with you, Bibring, and Singer there must be no dark corners. If there is no other way, I would rather drop the whole thing. I owe this both to myself and to you.

May 28

Today I received a reply to my letter, but an oral one. It was certainly not a direct answer because, although it was she who had made the appointment with me for eleven o'clock at the Anatomical Institute, I was forced to extract each and every word.

None of it was new to me—even though I did not know for sure, I had a definite presentiment. She had chosen between Bibring and me and decided on Bibring. She had been perfectly aware that it would hurt me every time she blatantly excluded me, and claimed that she did it intentionally because her knowledge of how I felt about her made my presence disturbing. When I countered that it had been her responsibility to open my eyes, she replied that she had been considering it for a long time. She had also asked Bibring to handle it, but he refused. Then I suddenly also understood why my relationship with Bibring was so peculiar. To call a spade a spade, it was pure jealousy, mutual rivalry, and this explains why I was disinclined to see his strong-points and sought out his weaker traits. I shall have to clarify matters with him as well.

However, I cannot say that this talk quieted me; on the contrary, it stirred up everything I had been hiding from myself for a long time. I am fond of the girl but, unfortunately, I lost. How shall I arrange our relationship now? Is the situation endurable? I think it is intolerable for all three of us.

June 5

Have now also spoken with Bibring.

We promised to be completely honest with each other from now on, and I am hopeful that this will greatly improve our relationship. Still, it is an unnatural relationship as things now stand among the three of us. I try to behave as naturally as possible and yet I sometimes become extremely annoyed at my own reactions. Last Sunday, Grete invited me on an outing. I struggled with the idea of not going, I had also not definitely accepted. However, at 2:30, when Bibring and I arrived at the Liebenberg Monument, somewhat late, we were informed by her sister Rosl that she had stayed at home to study and had requested that Bibring visit her. There was nothing especially peculiar about this, but I was absolutely furious. More than anything else, I felt like making an immediate about-face, although that would not do because of the others.

Why was I so angry? Even if she had come along, I would have had to do without her company! After all, am I still such an "ardent stripling" that just the presence of the lady of my heart is enough for me? I have tried to escape these thoughts, tried to imagine every possible bad trait Grete has—but unfortunately without success. This also disturbs my work, a condition which unsettles me most of all. So I do love her; otherwise, it would be impossible to be so totally preoccupied with thoughts of her and so tormented by unrest when I know: now *he* is with her!

June 24

I had hoped for so much from my talk with Bibring, but the situation, which for a while had apparently improved, has degenerated. I am beginning to doubt myself and my ability to live with people. Certainly a major portion of the blame rests with him, or both of us, or neither of us. Perhaps it cannot be otherwise, because of our relationship to the third party.

What is causing my constant inner disquiet, *this lack of a desire to participate*, this withdrawal into my own shell, this hatred for my environment? Yes, I hate everything and everyone, I shake my fists (albeit in my pockets, out of cowardice!) at everything that goes against my will, I pass arrogant judgment on people with whom I have hardly exchanged a word. When I go on an outing or am supposed to mingle with people under other circumstances, I always think: What will you do, what will you say, because you can't just sit there without saying anything if you don't want to look stupid. And I do not want to look stupid, because *I am not*. Whence this self-doubt? Whence my disapproval of those who talk a lot and my high opinion of those who are as taciturn as I? Is it jealousy? I am currently feeling very sluggish, I cannot bear my present life-style any longer. I would like to work, study, fathom certain areas of knowledge—and am hindered at every attempt by the petty issues of daily life. When I consider what I do on a given day (for example, today, June 24, 1919), I find very little which is purposeful but much that is exhausting. 6:30–9:00 tutoring; 9:00–11:00 lectures; 11:00–11:15 sat reading the newspaper in Votivpark; 11:15–11:45 waiting on line at the student cafeteria; 11:45–12:15 spent in the cafeteria's noisy rush and turmoil, a practically inhuman environment; 12:30–1:30 tutoring; 2:00–3:30 tutoring (chemistry); 3:30–6:00 wanted to do dissecting but had to stand in line at university offices until 6:00; 6:00–6:45 waiting on line, dinner, and now I am so tired that I am no longer capable of serious mental work. Where is the time *for me, for me, for me*? And so it goes, day in, day out. I have only two hours in the evening to study, and even then, frequently either the lights or my brain fails.

And you expect me to be happy, merry, gregarious? I was *once* highly capable of this. Can you understand me and my situation, you happy people, Bibring, Grete, Singer, etc.? You who have the entire day *to yourselves*, at your disposal, for your joy and pleasure. True, there are hundreds of people in my situation, but a person's tolerance, his memories and aspirations also exert an influence. And Grete had to cross my path under such circumstances, where my defeat was predetermined from the outset, leaving me not a moment's peace or quiet.

Aug. 19 and 20, Vöslau, at Winia's house

It would be a beautiful area if it weren't for . . . the women; the air would be refreshing if it weren't for the smell of their sweat. So many women, so little charm! All these fat monsters in dirndls. Can you imagine that: fat legs, trudging gait, breasts bulging out of cheap bodices, thighs squashed together, unaesthetic and unappealing, chattering (mostly Jewesses). (I didn't see one real man, just seventeen- to eighteen-year-old boys posing as "gentlemen.")

Dirndls ought to be worn by young, fresh girls, slender as reeds—and not by these sides of beef! Disgusting!

Sept. 1

Fredzio's engagement party! Who would ever have thought it could happen. Fredek, Mr. Frivolous, who never once in his life even thought of love, who always found the word empty and ridiculous, Fredek has fallen in love with a charming Hungarian girl, whom he had helped so that she and her family could come to Austria during the communist era. I told him that he didn't deserve her, for she is a perfect beauty, eighteen years old. I had no opportunity to satisfy myself as to her intellectual abilities.*

The liquid refreshments were of course excellent and the engagement party finally ended in a drinking bout at the Trocadero Bar.

Why is it that I can never be completely happy? By early evening, a feeling of emptiness and forlornness had crept over me, and when it came time for everyone to extend their congratulations, I broke into tears. This seemed ludicrous to me, but I did not try to suppress them. The thought "Father is not here" was constantly on my mind, and finally I fled to the bath-

---

*[Added in July 1920] Not a whole lot there. Two of a kind!

room, where I could allow my feelings free reign without disturbing the others.

Everyone was nice, the only one who irritated me was Marie with the big earrings and the showy diamonds on her fingers. I was relieved that I did not have to greet her or say goodbye.

We arrived home at two in the morning with the feeling of having spent a happy day.*

Sept. 6

My female colleagues are whores who haven't fallen yet (but would like to), and eighty-five percent of my male colleagues are idiots, boring everyday people, sensationalists.

Sept. 13

Proposed a topic for Grete to report on in the sexology seminar; namely, Strindberg's and Weininger's misogyny. I wonder what she thought of that?

Sept. 15

First analytic session: psychic homosexuality—compulsive act: having to walk quickly, the fear of missing something.

Sept. 17

There was a card tacked to my bulletin board in the Anatomical Institute from a certain Helene G. re chemistry. She asked that I come to see her on Thursday at four o'clock.

Rang her bell at 3:45. The thought crossed my mind as to whether I should charge fourteen kronen an hour as originally planned or fifteen kronen (considering the pension in which she lived). "The young lady is not home yet." Since I had a quarter of an hour to wait, I strolled up and down the street.

Daydream: I find here a female colleague exactly to my liking with whom I could study. She is young, intelligent, pretty, etc.

*[Added in July 1920] Atavistic fool!

At four o'clock, I rang again several times. A voice which did not exactly thrill me answered and asked me to wait a moment. A few minutes later (to my horror), a fat, giddy Jewess appeared who had one of those typically Galician faces! She extended her hand in an ungraceful gesture. Her dressing gown was buttoned carelessly and through the openings a red-and-green-checked slip could be seen. The room was small and dirty, the bed (at 4 p.m) was not made (ugh, for fourteen kronen!). Her first question: "You speak Polish?" "No, only German," I lied. "I passed physics and biology with honors and want to do well in chemistry, too." "Well, that will also depend upon you. My fee? Fourteen kronen." "That's as much as a professor charges." "I'm sorry, that is the value I place upon my time." "You know *vhaaat*? I will pay you a flat rate (am I a laborer? I asked myself). You prepare me for the exam and I will give you, say, two hundred kronen." "No, I cannot agree to that. But if the price is too high, I could simply acquaint you with the most important facts of chemistry," etc., etc.

Isn't life in daydreams more beautiful and glorious than in reality?

No word about Poldi until this moment, when I have the feeling that the relationship must be over.

Why did I forget to mention her, particularly in a diary? She, who gave me so many pleasant, happy hours—even if they were not so "lofty"! She is a dear, good girl from the working world, simple and nice, not like the others in this and related vocations. And therefore I spoke to her in the garden one lovely evening in May (the first time I had ever done this) and soon we were good friends. She candidly told me about her first boyfriend, the son of a wealthy man who owned a villa in H. Her voice betrayed no great guilt. We went on outings, rowboating, where she was always the center of attention. We got along magnificently, her simplicity and pleasantness attracted and held me. I have always fled with a certain horror from the inflated intellectual atmosphere in which I lived into the arms of an uncomplicated, simply-geared mind where I could rest. When we were lying in the Wiener Wald or somewhere else out in the country and I let her tell me things (usually just girl talk), and her wonderfully petite, white, well-cared-for hands fed me candies or spread plump sardines on bread for me—those were the times when I felt comfortable, stared wide-eyed for hours up into the blue skies, and thought of—nothing! Never did she ask me why I was silent, never did she complain or solemnly declare that she "loved" me. This last trait attracted me to her especially.* One word about love from her lips and I would have been gone forever! One person might call it vile, animalistic egoism—another might say, "How eccentric."

Remaining silent; but a gradually dawning awareness that "You would not be understood if you did try to say something" made me pity her lack of intelligence—later I missed it and now it's all over. The tale of the simple soul and the culture-afflicted individual is simply a myth. Poldi's simplicity and kindness is worth more than a hundred scholars.

Lia!!!† Is she a person with kindness and intelligence? She does have simplicity!!

Oct. 1919

Am studying the brain with Lia almost every day. In reality, I am losing time and trying to talk both her and myself out of these misgivings by claiming that I learn much more through teaching others. Is this true? No! It is clear to me that we enjoy studying together, but that's not all! Is she aware of this? Perhaps. In a dream which I foolishly analyzed for her, she disclosed her fear of an "intellectual danger," for she is erotically bound to a "boyfriend." When I revealed the latent content of the dream, she was obviously embarrassed, and even more so when she realized that the analysis was correct.

*[Added on June 12, 1920] Typical! Knave!
†Lia Laszky—a fellow medical student, whom Reich met while studying anatomy. [Eds.]

Oct. 1

Eleven o'clock. A young couple is standing at the trolley stop with their little five-year-old daughter. The child slips her hand through her father's arm and cries out, "Mommy can go to America! I've got my boyfriend right here!" Now what, you pure, chaste, asexual individuals!?

Oct. 3

7 a.m. at the Volkscafé, where I study with Bibring every day for the final anatomy examination. Several elderly ladies are having their morning chat: rising prices, when will things get better?, etc. A high-school teacher is discussing communism with a chimney sweep (who is already black with soot at seven o'clock). Rough simplicity pervades the small dark room, as if there were no sham or sordidness in the world.

Nov. 18

Speak:

To lie low behind a mask is "good"!

To stand firm without a mask is—beautiful.

But what to do if scraps remain on your face of that mask which you were unable to tear off?

To desire and to be able!

"Be yourself!"

With whose helping hand?

Search as you hobble along—there can be no help before you have found yourself!

This is what I wrote Lia for her birthday. Egocentric again!

Ha! I can already hear her shrill laughter:

"Oh! How sentimental!"

Not you, Lia—not Grete—not you, XYZ!

Not all of you together, but rather you within me must hope "to tear the shabby mask from your face"!

Life with others!

Am I searching for it?
No! But actually, yes!

Dec. 21

I love only "simple" people!

The complicated souls who deliberately weave the strands of their personalities over a wide span, for whom being complicated is an end in itself, are the people who entice one to waste energy needlessly in trying to understand them—and then what? Before you realize it, you are like the overcurious fly who negotiates two or three strands of the spider's web and then hangs there —struggling.

I am again suffering terribly from daydreams which prevent me from doing any work.

Twice I masturbated while consciously fantasizing about my mother—saw and felt only her abdomen, never her face. If I continue like this, I will very shortly wind up with Jauregg.* Ever since I wrote those lines to Lia, I have had no peace. Have not spoken with her since my examination. Does she know that it was I who sent the book? What went through her mind when she read those lines? Am I not an obtrusive, miserable person who disturbs other people's peace by making wry faces? In order to be interesting? No! I want peace, peace! I am crazy about Lia, I know it, am trying to resist. *I tried to warn her by interpreting that dream. I* tried to warn *her*!

But where do our paths cross? She is a human being! And what about me? Am I capable of nothing but cramming for exams and working for the seminar? And why?

Bibring said today: "People are extremely interested in you," "want to help you," "but if you cannot be helped?"

Why am I the one to be so—bad! Bad, yes, envious! Is it my

*Julius Wagner von Jauregg (1857–1940)—Austrian psychiatrist and neurologist. Best known for malaria treatment of general paresis, for which he received the Nobel Prize. [Eds.]

fear of my own miserable ego, the fear of not being able to hold out? Is that absolutely the only reason?

When I went to the opera with Lia, I felt something within myself drawing me into another sphere, a different realm, something strange to me—I wanted to speak, but my voice got caught in my throat; I felt a fool and once that happens, it's all over!

Swarowski * was waiting in front of the opera house and took Lia's arm as if it were the most natural thing to do! I was so flabbergasted that I was transfixed, was unable to move and made a strained effort not to betray my feelings. I immediately took my leave as she remarked, "I do hope Bibring brought the flour along!"

Disdain! I heard its shrill sound but said nothing, bit my lip! I and the flour, *Swarowski and Lia* (arm in arm). After the opera!

What was going on, clinically? Had she lied to me? Or did she have two "friendships"? The "arm in arm" really didn't look like "friendship" at all!

Are people so false—or am I a person who cannot understand this kind of thing?

Where shall I find peace! Where is there a little happiness?

Am I condemned never to leave my objective sexological learning behind, never to experience subjectively?

Dec. 27

Schmuck! And this is how it happened:

I arrived to take Lia to the Philharmonic. Since she was just having lunch, I spent a few minutes in her room. She entered, showed me all the things she had received for her birthday, and also mentioned the book *Mahler*, which "someone" had given to her along with a "note" slipped inside. She said that the note contained something that she already knew by heart—then she quoted the entire note. I: "That is completely incoherent!" She: "No, not at all! The person involved seems to know me very well, since he gave me the book on Mahler, and everything he

---

*Hans Swarowski—a musician who later married Lia Laszky. [Eds.]

wrote also agrees with the way I am. He did not disguise his handwriting; the whole note appears to have been written in one stroke—there is not one single slip of the pen."

I: "And aren't you trying to find out who wrote it?"

She: "Oh, no! It makes absolutely no difference to me, because the person is a schmuck! The people in my circle can speak to me directly. They don't need to resort first to anonymous presents and notes. At any rate, I think he must be a person who is not close to me but has observed me well and has no confidence in himself."

Did you hear that? Did you take it to heart? *You are a schmuck!* I've known it for a long time, so it does serve me right! But to hear it from her—that really did hurt!

"You are healthy, but there are also sick people in this world!"
"Yes, indeed! I am sick as well, but I recognize sickness in others!"

And then I had second thoughts: maybe she knew who the sender was, after all! I had written her two letters and did not disguise my handwriting to the point that she would have had difficulty recognizing it. Does she think she can express her opinion of me better this way?

I once asked her why she was playing "hide-and-seek," and in reply she wrote: "I am not in the same place as you are." Unconsciously (or consciously?), she said much more with this remark than she had perhaps originally intended. How greatly our paths diverge!

She is healthy and spontaneous, fathoms the profound depths of art with heart and soul, assimilates their effect within herself—she forms herself, educates herself to higher goals through the senses of sight and sound.* Doesn't her behavior during the performance of an opera or a piece of music speak volumes?

How easy to excuse her unproductiveness when it is judged by the criterion of objective value. The soul within her is not slippery or slimy but fresh, serious, and introspective. A soul that does not spread itself thin but rather seeks the depths!

---

*[Added in November 1920] What rot!

And I? Granted, I am productive in my way. I have a task, but it is one I am prepared to make my life's work—the psyche! The fact that this leads me into unclean depths which are unfit for society is also beautiful, grand—but where does that leave me? Where is the object of my soul, my slimy, slippery soul which struggles to attain dry ground? Is it the male-female problem again?

And still, she did not misunderstand what I wrote. But *I* should not be telling *her* all this; *she* should be telling *me*, screaming it into my ears a hundred times over: "Search as you hobble along—there can be no help before you have found yourself."

Jan. 6, 1920

Was at Lia's yesterday at five o'clock.

At first the conversation was sluggish and moved in the kind of channels usually caused by embarrassment. She deplored her conflict: medicine, for the sake of being productive, versus art, with which she really identifies. She was to reach a decision by the tenth about whether she would give up medicine; and she was still pondering the question: what then?

She asked me whether it was true—as so many people claim to have observed—that she had been acting arrogantly recently. I had to confirm this and remarked that she impressed me as being *surrounded by an iron band which prevented unwanted individuals from entering her sphere.* I told her that she was a mixture of emotional dullness and exuberance, with the latter constituting her inherent nature. She employed her dullness, I continued, to protect herself from communicating when she was in a state of exuberance, although this exuberance was excited only by the good or the beautiful. In order to prove this, I claimed, with an assurance which astounded even me, that in her life the ultimate in evil had never succeeded in having as lasting an effect on her as the ultimate in beauty.

For her, art is life, albeit a passive one; anyone who has no feeling for art is one-sided. I am one-sided. I inquired why her behavior toward me had changed so drastically and asked her to tell me the real reason, reminded her of how we had promised in the first days of our acquaintanceship to enrich each other and how she had gladly agreed to help me to understand art from the vantage of cognitive theory.

Her answer testified to the fact that two individuals of the opposite sex, each of whom has his own distinguishing "ethos," can not remain neutral after being together for a while. In order to prevent this shift, she had forsaken her original promise and intentionally altered her behavior. I confessed my present embarrassment frankly and declared that I had written that nonsensical note, which she will never be able to understand until she has become acquainted with my failure to find myself. I wanted to call her attention to the scene after the opera which had been so horrible for me and tell her of my jealousy when we were interrupted by Swarowski.

What will happen now? It can only be "either ... or"! The "or" is impossible and therefore ... !

Feb. 19, at the student cafeteria

I, a sexologist, become as embarrassed as a child when a girl behind the counter, with black eyes and a large shock of hair, winks at me and accepts another food ticket from me "as a favor."

You see your life in your work, and yet every minute of basking in the sun amid a dozen three-year-olds fills you with bliss. You preach that only positive, productive accomplishment is important—not the sacrifice of emotional sensuality to sonorous stimuli of unknown origin—and you long for a moment of nonproductivity, nonachievement, for one second of lazy idleness!

Is it the sun?! I think it's more!

What is life?

Lia! Are you more than you appear to be, or do you appear to be more than you are?

(Why does man always seek the most complicated answers when the simplest ones are the most probable?)

March 26

A mild spring evening is capable of dissolving plans formulated over months of mature consideration and replacing them with recent feelings.

How can the relationship of two people change simply because, through unnecessary, unintentional, and above all unwise deepening of that relationship, very fine sensitivities have been stimulated which, much against the will of the individuals involved, cause irresistible tension and relaxation that the participants are hardly aware of. A foolish, impertinent notion plays the lord, and a jumble of misunderstandings play the vassals.

June 13

"I am a dear, good person"!

Well, Lia, how did you suddenly arrive at that conclusion? Was it my letter, or my "suicide attempts"? After all, what do people know about me, and who told you this lie? Moreover, who could be interested in telling such stories about me? It would make absolutely no difference to me, if I did not have reason to fear that your sudden change of mood is due to these reports!

You want to learn to draw, Lia! I wish you much luck and happiness, Lia! But for a moment it pained me to hear that you no longer wish to study medicine—how I had looked forward to being allowed to help you, how interesting I wanted to make these studies for you, how I wanted to show you the depths which would have made the burden of an otherwise dry science easily bearable! "Let us enjoy art and the human being together." Yes, Lia, let us do that! But, Lia, I am desperate, I know so little, you will have to give me so much. Will you be able to muster the patience, will I not be bothersome to you? Unless I separate myself from my own profession completely when I am with you—can I succeed in that? "I must not fall in love with you!" Well, I do not know what it means to be in love, I also feel that

I am much quieter now. Yesterday I thought for a moment that our situation would be all the more beautiful and free—but that would be different from love produced unconsciously, love which would break through someday. Lia, let me say one thing to you and to myself right here and now: *I will not allow you to remove yourself from my world altogether.* It is my wish that we lend each other mutual support—but I am so afraid, Lia! What will the outcome be? It is a dangerous game . . .

Today is the last day of a week of music. I heard Mahler (Third and Fourth Symphonies), Beethoven (Ninth Symphony), the Schubert B minor, Mozart, Brahms, Schönberg (*Gurrelieder*), and a Fux Mass.

June 22

There was a symposium on the theme: Does man live from without or from within? It was held by Otto Fenichel at the residence of Hans Heller.

Intellectual and scientific arguments were to be excluded, only emotions were to be voiced (if indeed these can be expressed in words at all)—my dear Otto F., where did you go astray?

Milieu, course of events, initial impressions: A downright frighteningly elegant apartment. When we arrived, the ladies and gentlemen were just having dinner, a maid (or domestic servant) in a blinding-white apron dutifully offered to take my topcoat. Otto F., Desö,* and Lore Kahn† were already there. Otto and I played Ping-Pong for half an hour in a room which was apparently especially furnished for this purpose. Soon the others arrived, Otto's sister and her husband, Paul Stein and Gisl Jäger, several people from the Youth Movement, and Willy Schlamm.‡ We convened at eight o'clock and Otto began.

Shall I write down what he said? No, for I cannot! Let each

*Desö Julius—a Hungarian student who had escaped to Vienna in the summer of 1919 after the fall of Bela Kun's government. He introduced Reich to the communist movement. [Eds.]

†A young woman who was studying to be a kindergarten teacher. [Eds.]

‡Later, publisher of the *Rote Fahne* in Vienna. [Eds.]

person imagine some aspect of the evening's theme and he may be assured that he was also represented. Science, philosophy, the youth movement, but primarily politics provided fertile soil for genuine indignation, and the burning question of "how can we improve the situation" was voiced from all sides. Otto remained faithful to his intention of being emotional—he leapt from one subject to the next, was difficult to follow (he read from his notes), but one was able to respond as Otto had intended; i.e., one was carried along in a purely affective sense and shared his indignation. An obscure, indeterminate something began to ferment within me—and, I think, in most of the others as well. But, Otto, you made a mistake! If, as you said, it was not meant to be a scientific treatise, you should not have spoken for two and a half hours. *Emotions have no voice, lightning lasts only seconds.* Your words should not have been coals that glow for days but a sudden burst of fire. You should not have spoken for more than twenty minutes, and, my dear Otto, you overlooked one thing: in addition to the true pure flame of your ego there was something else that caused that fire to smolder. Lore Kahn remarked, "He wants to hear himself talk." But, Otto, this was also a way to introduce your good friends to your sister! In other words, you wanted—with the help of emotions—to show your sister how much indignation lies within you and your circle of acquaintances. No, Otto! *Emotions do not emerge on call! Not "Sunday evening at seven o'clock"!* They come and go when *they* please, and that was the *first* erroneous premise upon which you built.

And now to the *second* one! The intellect was supposed to be excluded, each person was to speak from his heart, the way people do in symposia! But then, for God's sake, there ought not to be discussions and debates on isolated issues! *After all, emotions cannot be debated!* We could not have expected to go home with a definite solution to the problem in our pockets. The only purpose of our meeting—communist and physician, lawyer and merchant, artist and member of the Youth Movement, philosopher and natural scientist—could have been to see the great, glaring misery *in all its colors*. But if the purpose of our meeting was misunderstood (or was it this very "purpose" which was so paralyzing?), then I shall apply the sharpest of criticism and tell you what paralyzed me (and, I am quite convinced, most of the others). Gradually, the discussion was sucked in by the tides of the *social* question. I am not acquainted with Hans Heller, but speaking from emotion, *I deny people who have never experienced even a moment's need any right to participate in discussions on social questions.* You may argue against this, I shall not try to substantiate it—it is simply an emotion! I am a skeptic, I had to learn to be distrustful and then to rejoice all the more when I was convinced that my skepticism was uncalled for.

The particulars? It would have been nicer if only you and Willy Schlamm had spoken. For example, Gretl Rafael inquired as to the *ethical* solution to the problem of who will want to do the lowly but necessary work when all mankind has come closer to the spirit. Paul Stein's answer was that of a *scientific, economic* socialist, and so the two spent half an hour missing each other's points.

You and Willy Schlamm were equally unable to reach an understanding. You defined the spirit in a scientific way as the will toward a problem and *its solution*. Willy Schlamm did not give the spirit any form whatsoever; he said, "it is undefinable," and this was completely correct from his subjective standpoint, as well as for us on that particular evening.

We all know—no, we *feel*—what the spirit is when we see a student-fraternity member covered with fencing scars, an officer in shining boots, or when we are intoxicated by a piece of music. We all sense it and strive for it in our daily lives, each in his own way; we all work toward the one goal, whether on your premise, Willy's, or any other. For in the end this premise is solely determined by one's own ego, as is the path, whereas the goal has been predetermined.

Willy Schlamm is a genuine person! I have come to respect him highly, although naturally I have a lot to say against him from the standpoint of science. For example, on the question of whether the scientist who "stands outside of conflicts" also serves the spirit in some way. Emotionally, I am entirely on his side! How much easier it is for purely emotional people than for those who are simultaneously also scientists. For science must be unemotional. The products of science belong to the nonscientific, although subsequently even a scientist can occasionally use his scientifically produced results toward affective ends (*vide* psychoanalysis)! The scientist merely procures the actual facts, upon which and with which the artist and revolutionary then build. Whereas the revolutionary paves the way for the artist, science certifies the artist's accomplishments. By producing proof of their causal necessity, science alone is capable of verifying those accomplishments through factual data, but the artist himself will always remain the avant-garde of the spirit. Thus, Willy Schlamm is correct: the art of music is the example nearest at hand.

What I did not say: In one respect I am not in emotional agreement with him; namely, when he says that every individual is under the obligation to become a part of the whole in serving the *objective spirit*. Here I take Stirner's* position, as I did during the discussion (although my attempt to express myself consisted of timid comments and incomplete sentences, for I was too overwrought), and must say: No, I do *not* want to *serve*; I want to establish the spirit within me. If I do this, and everyone else does the same, then the objective spirit (in Schlamm's sense) will be present. I do not wish to create a new god and then have my individuality grovel before him, no matter what his name. I call for opposition to everything which is over me. I do not want to serve the community above all else (as do Paul Stein and Willy Schlamm) and then try to be myself. I reject this different mode of coercion from without, for if I render service to myself, it is done for the good of the community. All acts undertaken for my self-realization will contain, in themselves, the service pos-

*Max Stirner—a pseudonym for Kaspar Schmidt (1806–1856). German anarchist whose philosophy of complete individualism was embodied in his book, *Der Einzige und sein Eigentum*. [Eds.]

tulated by Schlamm. You can already see that I want to live from within! But you will also notice that in so doing I have drawn closer to your position: I also feel that a symposium (if it really merits the name!) might serve the spirit better than the most brilliant speech delivered to a blindly obedient mass by an enthusiastic revolutionary. For that mass would then be living from without and therefore resemble those individuals who have, for example, remained unresponsive to the inner urge to become human beings. This is the first type described by Schlamm: the petty bourgeois. There is no fundamental differentiation here: the next equally enthusiastic but more appealing reactionary will soon win such individuals for his cause (incidentally, this fact has been borne out by experience!).

May I, should I, therefore become a "hermit"? I say no! The hermit forfeits the possibility of the "influences from without," in whose absence "influence from within," the actual fortifier, soon becomes impossible. *Living "from within" means forming the world, that which is "not me," the way my spirit* (and the spirit of everyone else who has the same desires) *demands.*

July 9

All gibberish! Man flees from himself! All lies—even the best, most sincerely desired truth! How lonely I am, essentially! Some people hate me, others fear me; very few despise me, many esteem me—but where can I find unity, belonging, where shall I find acceptance for a soul with a consuming desire to give!?

Julius? A person I respect as I have rarely respected anyone —and yet! Otto F. is a child and inwardly too alien to me! Singer and Weissman I shall overlook. Bibring—how, after my recognizing the situation, could I ever adapt to a structure so contrary to mine?

Lia? How do I know whether she has what I am looking for? I love her, constantly bear all possibilities in mind, hope, wait —day by day, hour by hour—has a letter arrived? Why did you write her? You have the urge—do it! No—this calls for reserve! Why? What is the meaning of all this? Why may I not simply approach the woman, tell her everything, and demand a yes or a no? Why this torment?

There are days when I am intoxicated with myself and my potential, hours when I am full of a firm, clear desire to be myself. What? Nonsense! Today I glimpsed it in its entire horrible scope: the contents of life, will, self-realization—what are these? Empty phrases—lies, all of them; I am surrounded by a grinning, bleak loneliness. Certainly, I will become a good physician, will work, but for whom? For myself! Ha! How can I say that; even the paper grins up at me, asking, "Why are you soiling me?" This, too, is vanity, lies! Am I not writing with the half-conscious thought that this will someday be read—by whom? Why do I love Lia? Because she demanded that I not love her? Wherever I go, I am suddenly jolted by the thought: you could meet her at this very moment—this is how she will hold out her hand and smile; no, you must not be too friendly; otherwise, she will think . . . Lia, at every turn of the road, always Lia! But why—I don't want this! This bondage! Lia wants to do something that will repel me forever. Yes, let her! Where can I find a person to tell me whether I deserve to be in the state I am? Where is there someone who will advise me how to find my way out of this mess? How miserable I really feel—and now the thought occurs to me again that Lia will read this, but then she ought to know all of my knavery, even the fact that I thought: What connection do I have with her? If I am to see her, to speak with her and not have anything specific to say, then—quick, a means to hold her—offer to teach her English, with the cunning ulterior motive: that's the way you can win her, while telling myself that English is an urgent necessity, for Lia and I will someday want to have a look at the world. Fool! Art, yes; music, but without Lia, insanity threatens me; death, which robs the mother of her child—I see it every day— why does it move me so?

How well I can lie! Asceticism—I do not practice it but am coming to believe in purity; then follows despair—it will come to naught, after all—a night excursion, defilement, and even the compelling desire to do it again. She is a child, loves me; and I, rogue that I am, dare to pursue her even while thinking constantly of another. Am I now considering calling it off? Lord forbid, it is all a lie! Is there some other way? Who is different, show him to me so that I can learn from him, find support! At this moment, how beautiful it would be to fire the big army revolver! But here, too, I am lying to myself, for even as I write this, the deed is out of the question.

Outside, the wind is howling, that rushing which made me shake in my bed as a child, made me look out into dark stormy nights with horror—Mother! How gravely you sinned! Would it be a help to have you here today? What a howl. I am sitting with my back to the window, gooseflesh—oh, I am educated: musculi erectores pilorum (or pilarum)—covers me time after time, but I remain sitting, freezing; no, I am shaking from it, here it is again! Desolate, deserted, confused—loneliness! Aha! it just occurred to me: I once remarked that I am happiest when I'm alone! Ridiculous! Coward! Liar! Lia!

Shame! How sentimental all this is! What if I read it again years later. How cold it left me—or was I actually happy?— when I read about Steinach's* attempts at rejuvenation! How long do you want to live, fool? The revolver just came to mind again. I'm frightened now, now I'm shuddering, I'm tired, want to sleep—but vanity, keep on writing until you pass out, writing, writing. Steinhof,† an opportunity to study schizophrenia. Let Austria and Germany unite, "fulfillment of this order to be reported by official notice"; we read that today, and how we laughed! We laughed, haven't laughed that heartily for a long time. I'm tired, but no, Rita wants me to bring a copy of Weininger to her at the tennis court, then Julius is coming for me, we'll study, then the cafeteria, then sleepiness? Work? The Danube? Get a suntan? Vanity—then the seminar, we are supposed

*Eugen Steinach, M.D.—professor of physiology at the University of Vienna, experimented with sex-gland functions and sex hormones, particularly with regard to rejuvenation. [Eds.]
†A Viennese mental institution for chronic cases. [Eds.]

to publish the lectures, how proud I am, I will write a good paper. Oh no, another one in addition to *Peer Gynt*.* Do you think I'm a nobody? Strange, these ideas: Lia will certainly read this and think I'm raving mad, to love a madman is madness in itself. But I was never as sane as I am now, no, truly never! Ugh! I am so disgusted, waves of disgust are choking me. The Future! How long—why, a full five pages! And nothing but thoughts that occur to a person when he sits naked, shuddering and shaking (again and again, now), with his back to the window at 10:30 p.m. The wind is howling again—no, it's the trolley! What is going on in Vienna at this moment: people getting drunk, bodies wildly intertwined, everywhere, from the ground floor to the top—do I want it, too? Yes or no? Man, take a stand—yes or no?! Is that it? Impossible, and yet . . . ! Why don't you go to a prostitute? Ha, it *disgusts* you! Easy, easy—I'll wait, I want to wait, wait and study pathology, wait and pass the exam in internal medicine, wait and graduate, wait, for what? How exhausted I am! I am acting out a comedy for myself. Beware: Lia will read this. All right, how does this comedy differ from the large-scale one we experience every day? What good is all this?

Come on now, stop writing!

Lia, I fear your arrival!

Desö still calms me down every time, without even knowing it—with what assurance he looks to the future, how euphoric he is when he imagines a European communist state emerging in just a few months! Have you any idea that blood will be shed, must be shed? I am moving more and more toward the left; there is only one solution: not overcoming or bypassing the Hydra but destroying it, grinding it to dust! How frequently one hears the opinion (and how easily one arrives at it) that persuasion is useless—calcified brains are irreparable! Break them, smash

---

*"Libidinal Conflicts and Delusions in Ibsen's *Peer Gynt*." A lecture Reich would deliver on October 20, 1920, as a candidate for membership in the Vienna Psychoanalytic Society. Included in *Early Writings, Volume One* (New York: Farrar, Straus and Giroux, 1975).

them, and brutally sever even the weakest links with the past, even with your brother, should he not follow you.

I profess to want a revolution but am not a revolutionary, I want the whole but despise the particulars—politics disgusts me! May I consider it sufficient that I constantly, hour after hour, inspect, examine, and correct myself? Yes, indeed! I fear that this is also a performance of the contemporary comedy of narcissism—what, then, is real? My life is revolution—from within and from without—or it's comedy! If I could only find someone who has the correct diagnosis! But if it occurs to me personally that it's comedy, then that must be correct! (Oh, I don't give in that quickly!) The life I am leading can be examined objectively; other people have also arrived at my conclusion. Does that mean that everyone who is like me is also acting out a comedy? What about our secret thoughts which surface so rarely? I don't remember, or I don't want to remember?

Thus, I arrive at the decision to remain in this role even if it is a comedy, for if I am to be a good actor, I must exert all my strength; the role demands to be internalized. The effect remains the same—if I never show my real face. What a miserable human being I am! All my emotions, my rage, my anger, all I do, and all I am is a lie—or all these stupid scribblings are blissful masochism! Who could pick up the thread in a mess like this? I remain as I was, but such excursions cannot fail to be useful and will therefore be undertaken frequently.

July 12

A look back offers magnificent insights!

Man is an animal of the moment!

Man? No, me! Where do I get the nerve to generalize!

What a role women play in my life! Not one mention of my work anywhere! *Sexus, sexus*—the dominant factor!

July 21

Those dull moments! They do occur. You resist them because they cast a shadow over the greatest beauty, but a night spent in the company of bedbugs is stronger than all your resistance. Do you know them, those hours when the great question "Why?" and the amazed "How was it possible?" paint your whole world in drab colors and the things you love or hate, or that don't even matter, all go up in the smoke of paralyzing indifference? That is the way I feel as I write this; I move my pen without thinking, slowly; tired, dull, drab—and how has it come about? I am not joking: I was bothered by bedbugs all night long.

This morning I felt the urge to apologize to Desö for the ecstatic remarks I made on the Grosser Kanzel. They now seem stupidly out of place to me, although at the time they met with everyone's approval. I had touched upon something inside them and myself; how strange I felt! Naturally, I had often entertained such thoughts, but I had never had so clear an awareness of them! Perhaps I now understand my halfheartedness on a number of issues. Wasn't the situation made to order for an eruption? But why does it now seem so peculiar to me? What sacrifices must one make to mundane existence?

It was about midnight and we were lying close to the edge. Our eyes beheld only the heavens arched above us, frightening, overpowering, with their innumerable lights. Our ears heard only the rushing of the wind past the sharp mountain ledge, that deeply melodic, prolonged, mournful whistling, unique and inimitable, which has always moved me—and moved the others as well. Our bodies did not feel the raw cold of midnight at a high altitude, for our eyes were on the starry heavens. And while I bore no concrete thoughts in mind, Desö jumped up, walked to the edge, and said in a composed voice, "Is it believable that right now, at this very moment, communists and capitalists— or rather, their slaves—are at each other's throats in Poland?" He, the sober revolutionary who consumes every newspaper every day, whose existential core consists of economic and party issues—it was he who asked the question!

And all at once the gist of my thoughts became clear to me, climaxing in the recognition of my egocentric attitude toward daily life—in figurative terms: eyes to the ground—and in the recognition of my present, partial sense—since I had lifted my eyes from the ground—of being a microcosm in contrast to the starry macrocosm. How often do we humans really view the sky? So miserable are we that we are *not even capable of reliving the intellectual experiences of such a night.* At best, an emotional trace of that night remains, but not the experience itself which sustained the emotion (or if the experience does remain, it is ridiculously distorted). And I cried out: *"Call them here, all those who are slaughtering each other, and every one of them will collapse in the presence of this beauty; all imagined grievance must—I say must—vanish in this rushing wind!"*

"They are fighting for their lives and for bread!" shouted Desö; suddenly he had again become the Desö I knew from the café.

I: "Can you judge the significance of an anthill and the struggles that go on there?" It was obvious that this comparison was completely out of proportion.

He: "It is the great revolutionaries who *cause* the uprising!"

I: "Seen from our standpoint, yes. But I am trying to . . ."

No, it's impossible! Cannot be put down in words at this desk, at this moment! That would only ruin everything.

Aug. 1

Wrote Lia before I went hiking, answered her short note. I am afraid that I have once again caused much damage, I asked her to watch her step (what right did I have to do that?). What do I know of her? And how much she knows of me! Must not this imbalance have an effect? I wrote to her about my yearnings and their meaning for me, but not about their contents. Today, two weeks before her arrival, I am exhausted by yearning! By what right does she keep her balance? Why should she be allowed to possess the innermost part of me this way, as she does! Perhaps I am mistaken in her. Would it be good for me to find out? I don't know her at all, but I do love her! How will she seem to me now after this long absence? The hiking relaxed me; I dove right into my work, which I had been unable to face for a long time. Now I long for work and music, am looking forward to the events of the coming winter, and also, for the first time in a long, long while, to my externship at the hospital, my lecture at the Psychoanalytic Society—but I am taking my time, another two hikes, I will store up my energy, and then—work. It does not seem so drab anymore. At this moment, I almost feel capable of happiness. It came over me again today: *there are so very many things which are better, more attractive, than party politics*! I almost allowed Desö to bowl me over. My life, my actions, are dominated by one idea: *reality is dirty. How the communists revile the Social Democrats—disgusting! They attacked the Social Democratic labor council like a pack of mad dogs because of one action; in other words, they act exactly the way the Christian Socialists do. And the Social Democrats? The same!* Ugh! Yes, if one could only find a group that *functioned outside of the mire of political machinations, which always, no matter where they originate, bear the stamp of power and egotism. Such groups must be brought into existence!* They must grow in spirit!

Aug. 7

I outdid myself prematurely in my search for other lonely beings—I am, by far, not secure enough to be able to give up my own position. I am alone again. Julius is growing cold; he has his own circles where people can join him in songs of rejoicing over every step forward the Russians make—as if happiness dwelt for certain in that. In promoting socialism, people still refuse to see that two reigning but irreconcilable elements are present; namely, *economic communism* and *intellectual revolution*. Only the dictatorship of the proletariat can lead to the former; only a slow-maturing process of evolution leads to the latter. The one is guaranteed through the other. But do you think the situation would change if the latter were *lacking*?

Human intercourse needs amphimixis—or is this, too, merely a hideous generalization? I almost think I am incapable of offering anything in the long run—or, better said, I feel that a state of concord would have to prevail which as yet has not been put to the test. But doesn't this also deeply involve sexual matters? What, then, would be the duration of such a state? Complete mutual surrender, physical and emotional; common path and goals—is that sufficient?

The outside world disturbs me. I am myself in the work I am now completing—the thought of Lia is a disturbance! What does that woman want? What a fool I am! What is disturbing me this afternoon? Not simply the question of going or not going to the train station? Nauseating! That such thoughts should form the contents of an afternoon, and why? The outside world again. *If people were different, these thoughts would be unnecessary; one would either simply go or forget about it.* Ah, but strategy! No! I cannot, and even if it means losing everything! I have grown lax; I watch with horror as I slip back into the old stinking rut! Julius, Moser, Robert, Lia—with all of them I will carry it to the extreme: an ironclad yes or no! In any event, I will know that I am hard. Hard, ruthless, forthright. *Whoever is not strong enough to accompany me should stay where he is!*

Saw Julius! Today he said that he had been waiting for the District Workers Conference to reach a decision on Hungary; had the decision been positive, he would have fought along with them! Julius, how little you know about yourself! Nothing but big words! The very moment you try to move a single stone, the entire edifice collapses. I respect him as I respect few people, and therefore I should tell him.

Robert? I am afraid he will meet with a bad end! He should go to America, to the hardest possible school; he needs it! I must refrain from all attempts, but also from being softhearted toward him. You say he is my brother? Well, what is that supposed to mean? Perhaps that we understand each other less than if we were friends!

Lia? I am quieter now! Perhaps I am only wishing I were. Should we not reach an understanding when I remain *myself* and do not assume a pose, then it is all over and I will be more careful in the future.

Aug. 11

Lia arrived today. I sense it and am waiting; maybe she will visit me soon! What a poor fool you are! Where does this euphoria come from? From the fact that you helped her to surprise her family? That you ran her errands? Why didn't she want to "surprise" me, too? Why do I construe her request for help as a gesture of trust placed in me? There are two possibilities: If Lia is what she purports to be, a contemplative person, then the surprise could be viewed as consideration for her parents, a concession to their age. If I was the one she chose to let in on the secret, what is to follow?

If, however, she is not such a person, then she was aware that I would help her and used me as a means for *others who are dear to her*. What is the use of ruminating? I am afraid to see her again!

I am losing all my composure in my dealings with this woman, I vacillate between being myself and not being myself, don't know what to say or how to say it; I am inhibited, fear that every remark I make could be used against me. Is the fault within me, within her, or in the nature of sexuality? No matter how much they actually discuss *sexus* in scientific circles, the real, essential, decisive kernel in daily life always remains untouched.

I love this girl and can only recall one of her features, the full, soft contour of her chin. I love her mind—but if human beings can say so little about themselves, what are others to say about them?

I love the girl and *want to possess her*; what is the use of all this rhetoric? *But intellectual possession is necessary if the physical aspect is to be dignified and not become a source of disgust and boredom.* I wish she had the strength to think along the same lines. This mode of behavior is sound in itself, if only she responds to it. Are we intellectually compatible? What do I know about her? Each one of us is interested in individuality, that much is certain!

There are two types of desire-to-possess: one without regard for duration, and the other including duration. The first type can forgo an intellectual partnership, while the latter is impossible without it. Is intellectual partnership therefore only the means to an end? Or is it the actual issue? I know that by making the first assumption I am pronouncing my own sentence, but is what we desire identical in value with what already exists? Can man exceed his own limits?

Physicality may aid in strengthening intellectuality and vice versa! Is not the crown of the ego a double ego, which encompasses both? *It is my contention that whoever has saved his physicality from the quagmire need not fear the false shame of elevating it to a goal!*

Do I have a right to this goal? For a long time, I have at least been striving to achieve it.

Evening. I waited but nervousness got the better of me. At four o'clock I went to her house and stayed in the "family circle" until 7:30.

Lia has changed: physically she has blossomed; intellectually she's more womanly! Is this good? While she was unpacking her suitcases she twice remarked, "This or that will adorn X. when I marry!"

She inquired about the outing that was planned. I was particularly quiet, yes, even humorous. And then again: "I can't promise anything until I have telegraphed." Whom? Later I found out: Hans Swarowski. So it is still going on! I cannot take it any more!!

My high spirits, my heartfelt joy over her presence vanished; I was speechless, but through an extreme effort I succeeded in appearing outwardly composed. As usual on such occasions, I was overcome by feelings of insecurity.

Tomorrow she is going to pay me a visit. I cannot carry on!

Is the woman playing a game? Isn't she aware of anything? Am I no one? Tomorrow will see the end of it, one way or the other.

I will not allow her to play with me anymore! She must tell

me whether she loves Hans! She is obligated to do this after all that has happened.

Easy, just take it easy! Otherwise, you will lose everything! If only I weren't already tired from struggling with myself as well, so tired. Why do I take everything so tragically? I almost question whether this is genuine. But then what is genuine?

In any event, this is an intolerable situation. I *must* put an end to it!

I am still in a slump! Man, get moving! My soul cries out, writhes in painful craving for Lia! I don't want to tolerate that. What have you made of me, Lia? Disgusting that I must don a new mask! Oh, if she would only do something that would repel me, something horrible, radical—I am on the verge of cracking wide open.

No, I do not believe that this is falseness! Why should I writhe? I do not want to, no, no! Is there no escape? If I could only write down everything that is pulling me back and forth, leaving me no peace. Don't take it so tragically—fool! Yes, but what good does it do me if I only say it!

I DON'T WANT TO DIE!

No! How does that woman dare to make me think such thoughts! I will not, but I'm so very tired, I cannot carry on, it's been almost a year, isn't that enough!

I can't! I'm hysterical!

Woman, don't you see that there is a person here who is giving himself to you, honestly, completely, a person who cannot lie, ensnare, or entangle you—oh, if I only could! No, I will not! But why does it hurt me so not to be able to do it? "Your own responsibility, comrade!" But, Lia, it's no fault of yours. Forgive me! I am crying—shame, shame.

Aug. 15

1:30 a.m. I am not crying anymore! I am laughing, am happy—although not completely: *Lia loves me,* she told me, we told each other, although in a somewhat peculiar way which is giving me second thoughts. She is going to Hans, after all; she is his woman, after all! Lia, you were not frank with me, were false in some ways, although it was not your fault; you do not see yourself clearly!

Why did this victory, this forward surge have to be a half triumph, why can't I have all of Lia! Something is not right there—I fear her journey to Hans! Lia, I have firmly decided to be your support, one way or the other. You must "become"! I love you, Lia! But remove the last thorn, I do not like unfinished business, I want all of you, we should be able to give to each other, the iron band around you must be broken!

The time is ripe, I want to become one with you, you are to become my helper, my support, my second self!

Is it symbolic that the diary that I have been keeping for two years ends with the winning of Lia?

Well, then onward! Now I feel strength within me! I fear no one else, for I am able to help you! Through me, you shall become!

Diaries are the receptacles of filth!!

Not one word about Lore, who gave me true peace and joy!

Not one word on my scientific activities!

* * *

In 1920 there lived in Vienna a nineteen-year-old girl named Lore Kahn who was a kindergarten teacher. She was lively, clever, and somewhat "messed up" because she had no proper boyfriend. She was in love with a brave revolutionary politician who no longer belonged to the romantic Youth Movement. She had attached herself to him and slept with him. But now she could no longer have him. This made her miserable.

Lore became psychically ill, even though she was a strong person. She lost her self-confidence and became moody and so no longer liked herself. She came to me for therapy in the winter of 1919–20. She settled a few conflicts, among them the one with Karl Frank the politician, which was no longer so important to her. Added to this, she fell in love with me. It was not only a case of father-transference; and where, after all, is the basic difference between a genuine, sensual love for the father and the equally real sensual feeling for a lover who is to replace father and mother and simultaneously provide the pleasure of sexual union! In short, Lore declared one day that she was analyzed, and now she wanted me.

I did not feel much desire for her. One should not sleep with one's patients; it is too complicated and dangerous. But Lore was at last "herself." She could wait, she said. We met in the sexology seminar. She gave an excellent, lively report about kindergarten. This was also a little for my benefit. We were good friends. She invited me to go hiking with her. We hiked all over the Wiener Wald. In the evening we returned home singing. Lore had loosened her hair; she knew what she wanted and did not hide it. After all, she was no longer a patient. And it was nobody's business. I loved her, and she grew very happy.

On the 27th of October 1920, she wrote the last entry in her diary:

> I am happy, boundlessly happy. I would never have thought that I could be—but I am. The fullest, deepest fulfillment. To have a father and be a mother, both in the same person. Marriage! Monogamy! At last! Never was there coitus with such sensual pleasure, such gratification, and such a sense of oneness and interpenetration as now. Never such parallel attraction of the mind and body. And it is beautiful. And I have direction, clear, firm, and sure—I love myself this way. I am content as nature intended! Only one thing: *a child*!

Lore had a very dear and sensible mother. Her father was an honest tradesman. Her mother was sexually active, but she had never felt happiness and was therefore resigned. She experienced a little of her daughter's happiness vicariously. She had a brother who was moralistic and strict.

After the war, an affair of two young people without marriage was no longer a crime, but it was an embarrassment. It should end in marriage. Lore was young and did not want to get married. She only wanted to be happy monogamously and have my child. Pressure began to be applied quietly. For a long while, Lore said nothing; she rebelled against it. But she loved her mother. She did not want to "hurt her." So she finally spoke to me—very openly, humanly, as a friend. We were agreed that marriage would be madness. I was twenty-three, she was nineteen. We had everything *ahead of* us. To tie ourselves already? And to start to hate each other because of being tied? To renounce happy love with others forever? She knew that I loved Lia, differently from her. We understood that one can love two people simultaneously when one is young. She was not angry, any more than I was angry with Lia. All was well between us. But we had no room in which we could be together undisturbed. It was no longer possible at my place; the landlady had become hostile and a threat. So Lore got a room at a friend's. It was unheated and bitter cold. Lore became ill, ran a high fever, with dangerous articular rheumatism, and eight days later died of sepsis, in the bloom of her young life.

*　　*　　*

Nov. 20

A final letter

To you, Lore, with your now cold, pale face and its lingering smile at a world which your free spirit outwitted wherever it could; to you, with your loose flowing hair which you tossed into my face on a bright moonlit night as we danced our way home, hand in hand, blissful over our world; to you, who made me forget the sordidness of life by telling me tales such as only you could tell as I rested my head on your lap in the warm sunshine; to you, who awaited me in a dark room, whose tender lips kissed away all my cares in a happy onslaught and sowed the seed of lighthearted laughter within me! Your will to live, your sparkling joy in life were unable to frighten away an incredibly hideous death; how you smiled and overlooked the filth which surrounded you! I send you a kiss, my beloved companion. When all else has receded into the infinite grayness, your naïve, childlike freshness will still be with me. Perhaps each star which shone upon us will wipe away the revulsion which suffocates me.

I read in your diary where you wrote: "To have a father and be a mother, both in the same person." My dear, dear Lore! You were a mother-companion to me, a companion from whom I struggled away in the direction of a whore, but always returning to you, your peace, your love!

I do not beg your forgiveness; you were aware of everything and understood me, you, my mother—to whom I was a father as well! When freedom had just been achieved and our union just commenced, you met your death: am I doomed never to find happiness? Is this the universal fate of man? Poor, poor Lore! How you must be freezing out there, how icy cold it must be inside your six boards, my poor, good, little Lore! But no! As the priest blessed you, you were with me, standing at my right side—and you laughed, a fiendishly joyous laugh. Are you cold, Lore? Is it cold down there? You—and death! The last words in your diary were, "Only one thing: a child!" Why must the world be like this, to deny us a child, your child and mine, Lore!

Everything is so dismal! I want to immerse myself in work and forget that you have passed away—I want to keep your life, our life, alive in my heart!

In short, once again an all too clearly defined period of my life is over, *one* year, the richest, the most beautiful, and the saddest as well. I want to live through it again—let me review it briefly!

It began with the winter semester of the year 1919; the hustle and bustle of registration, enrollment, and the start of the seminar in sexology made the time fly. Otto left for Berlin and I was to take over leadership of the seminar. I knew that holding the seminar together had been easy for him but would be difficult and strenuous for me. I not only wanted to keep it going but *had* to. There was a lot of work, preliminary talks; I wanted to do my very best on all scores because of my great fondness for

Otto. I will not deny that it gave my ego a tremendous boost when, at the end of the spring term, I was chosen as the new chairman. But then I developed feelings of inferiority, and if the truth be told, I was not mature enough to assume the chairmanship, even if I did know more about sexual psychology than anyone else. And thus, to strengthen my position, I divided the seminar into a biological and a psychological group. I asked Eduard Bibring to preside over the first group, while I myself assumed leadership of the second. I should like to mention in advance that we did accomplish something, and when Otto returned home at Easter of 1920, I was able to report to him on an impressive number of good lectures.

Meanwhile, the time had also come to prepare for anatomy. Since I had to finish the work of three semesters that year, it was necessary to be ready for the comprehensive examinations by Christmas. On the second day of registration, our group from the year before—Grete Lehner, Eduard Bibring, Samuel Singer, and I (Weissman had not yet returned from Switzerland)—was already pushing and shoving its way into the prosector's office, where the cadavers for dissection were dispensed. Six candidates for the examination were assigned to each cadaver; we were lacking two people. Since we worked well, and quickly, but also wanted to be by ourselves, the choice of the additional two was no easy matter. Cadavers were only given out to complete groups, and those which were not complete had to wait and risk not being able to finish on time.

An acquaintance and his girlfriend, a hideous woman who hated me, were supposed to fill in, but she had not yet enrolled; thus, we had to search. Then, because I was farthest toward the front, Grete Lehner handed me two slips with the names of available students. As I was being shoved back and forth in the crowd, I read from the slips of paper and simultaneously called out to the assistant: "Resi Schwarz and Lia Laszky"! When I came out, Grete Lehner introduced me to our two female colleagues—actually, they were two girls—who had been standing in a corner of the hall. I greeted them briefly and then left.

Dissecting began. Bibring and I were working on the lower section, Laszky and Schwarz on the upper, and Singer and Lehner were doing the head and throat. I worked silently, as always, exchanging only brief comments with Bibring. Grete Lehner and Singer were forever rattling on; Resi Schwarz, a small, merry creature with soft features, was in despair over her lack of knowledge; Lia Laszky said nothing, only an occasional remark to Grete Lehner, with whom she had gone to high school. I first took a closer look at this new acquaintance when I received a self-confident, curt answer in response to instruction I gave regarding Laszky's area for dissection (she was working on my left). It occurred to me that she bore a great resemblance to another female colleague who had caught my attention in the lecture hall because of her thick blond hair and soft, full face. Lia Laszky, too, had a soft face, a small nose and mouth, blond hair—and could give one a very knowing look.

One day I was discussing the seminar with Bibring and informed him that Dr. Sadger* planned to give a course on psychoanalysis. The conversation gradually turned to that subject and Lia remarked that she had read only a limited amount of the literature. Since she asked me to lend her something, I offered to bring her a copy of Hitschmann† and invited her to the seminar on the coming Saturday. "Which seminar?" she asked. "The seminar in sexology." Somewhat surprised and somewhat curious, she promised to attend. (My report on libido concepts‡ was scheduled!) The next day, I brought her the book I had promised and made several comments on the peculiar attitude of the layman toward psychoanalysis. "Would you be willing to help me if there is something I don't understand?" "It would

---

*Isidor Sadger, M.D.—a pioneer in psychoanalysis, particularly interested in homosexuality and perversions. [Eds.]
†Eduard Hitschmann, M.D. (1871–1958)—Director of the Psychoanalytic Clinic in Vienna. Author of *Freuds Neurosenlehre* and studies on frigidity in women. [Eds.]
‡"Drive and Libido Concepts from Forel to Jung," included in *Early Writings*, *Volume One* (New York: Farrar, Straus and Giroux, 1975).

be a great pleasure!" was my conventional reply, while I simultaneously looked forward to being able to show off what I knew. An ensuing conversation on socialism brought us all closer together—I discovered that L.L. had been a member of the Wandervogel*; we had a slight argument, a difference of opinion. L.L. brought me a copy of Landauer's *Aufruf*.

L.L. attended the seminar; approximately thirty were present, most all of whom gradually left, thank God. My lecture had elevated me out of all proportion in everyone's eyes, since no one was able to follow it except a few members from the year before. And it was nothing but a simple report on Freud and Jung.

The next day, I entered the Anatomical Institute and saw L.L. sitting on the stone bench in the hall. It seemed to me that she was somewhat withdrawn. After a few casual remarks, she said, "I am not going to attend the seminar anymore!" "Why?" "I don't understand the material, and besides . . . I found it disgusting." I tried, as far as I was able after such a short acquaintance, to point out the reasons for her disgust—but without success: "What this involves is wallowing in filth, and I cannot participate!" Her participation was not extremely important to me, because I did not know her potential, so I let the matter rest.

But still, the incident had given me cause to speculate on the basis for her sudden withdrawal, on the fear which had spoken from deep within her.

We saw each other in the dissecting room, at lectures, and in the course on psychoanalysis, which had just begun. Since I was to take the anatomy exam in four weeks—i.e., at the end of December—and wanted very much to go over the structure of the brain with another person, I offered to study this subject with her. During this time, I was very busy: in addition to my medical courses, I also gave lessons in chemistry and physics—

---

*A movement of bourgeois youth, motivated by a half-conscious rebellion against the dullness of the parental home.

unwillingly, but compelled by circumstances. Furthermore, I was occupied with psychoanalysis in a most intensive way, not only due to an objective interest in this completely new science but also because of a vague sense that through it I might approach certain obscure regions of my own ego. I worked like an animal, was at it from 7 a.m. to ten o'clock at night; I withdrew from the world completely. Only rarely did I go to the theater or attend a lecture.

I had restrained my ambition (which was directed at fleeting satisfaction and was getting out of hand), correctly assessed the gaps in my education, and consoled myself with long-term goals. In addition to this, my financial situation was such that I was unable to keep up with the life-style of my fellow students, who were all more or less well off. Thus, I became a recluse, desired no contact with the community, and simply worked.

I visited L.L. and experienced the same thing I had experienced a hundred times before under such circumstances: her parents' tasteful, elegant, almost luxurious apartment and the rather distinguished, casual manner of her still young, attractive mother made me feel constrained—although the relationship did become cordial. Our anatomical studies went well, and I was pleased when L.L. remarked once that she had not imagined that anatomy could be so beautiful. She also visited me in my room, but our original enthusiasm for studying together waned, anatomy was replaced by conversations on a wide variety of subjects, and L.L. herself began to interest me, for her personality revealed a strong homosexual component. When I mentioned this frankly, she was at first amazed at my "knowledge of human nature" and then confessed that she had recently been passionately in love with a girl.

One day she remarked that she feared psychoanalysis, thought it must be horrible to experience one's own ghastly unconscious. Since I had been observing a growing affection for me in her eyes, her speech and gestures, I felt that the moment had come to draw her attention to this, for during the entire duration of our relationship I had not once entertained even a thought of a possible erotic liaison. I was so much a "sexologist" that I had even objectified my own sexuality. At the beginning of the winter, I had broken off a relationship with a working-class girl of whom I was very fond despite the fact that she could offer me no more than her love and her young body. The summer with its various amusements was over, and the prolonged get-togethers in cafés where one had to carry on a conversation on matters of no importance had become tedious.

Thus, I considered it my duty to warn L.L., especially when I discovered, in conjunction with my interpreting a dream (which I later regretted a thousand times), that she had a boyfriend in Munich.

One Sunday, we met in a café on the Ring. The morning passed in very productive conversation on the Youth Movement; I read her a letter from Otto and my reply to it. She announced a desire to organize a group for girls and gave a clever, carefully considered presentation of her plans. She told me about her school-days, the outings, the discord at home; her wish was to become independent as quickly as possible and then leave home. She had begun to study medicine only because it was her father's wish*; would have preferred music or drawing. However, since she had little self-confidence, as she put it, the issue was no longer important.

When we left, I accompanied her a short way and then suddenly remarked, "One other thing! I'm afraid I cannot study anatomy with you anymore. There isn't much time left before the examination and I still have a lot to do." Nevertheless, we were to stay in touch. (I had told her a lie; I had just as much time as before.) We parted good friends.

Bibring and I decided to take the exam before Christmas (i.e., in three weeks) and studied together every morning from seven to ten o'clock and every evening from eight to ten. Despite the increased work load, I did not cease my other activities: in the afternoon I had two analytic sessions; in the evening there was

---

*Lia's father was a physician. [Eds.]

Sadger's course. L.L. sent me one patient whom she claimed was a homosexual although I could find nothing but a compulsion neurosis. During the course of treatment, this patient mentioned a certain Hans Swarowski, whom he raved about and praised as a magnificent person. One evening L.L. appeared at Sadger's course with a young man with whom I immediately fell in love; never before had I seen such delicate, spiritual features in a man. As I discovered later, it was Hans Swarowski. Since I was not keen on the company of a third person, I did not accompany her home that evening.

One morning—it was still very dark outside (about 6:30 a.m.)—I left my building with a coat draped loosely over my shoulders and headed for the Volkscafé across the street, where Eduard Bibring and I usually studied together. I had not yet crossed the street when I noticed a female figure coming down the Bergstrasse: it was Lia Laszky!

I was surprised but said nothing, and we entered the Volkscafé together. She informed me that she had just come from the university, where she had put her name down for opera tickets; at eight o'clock she had to go back. We talked of inconsequential matters; for example, how fine it was that I could study in the Volkscafé, etc. Soon Bibring arrived and for a moment I became embarrassed: how to explain her presence to him? In order not to disturb us, she moved to another table. I felt like holding her back and deferring our studies, but said nothing and appeared so confused that Bibring murmured to me, "Try not to look so embarrassed!" Just before eight o'clock, she left.

Some time later, in the dissecting room, a fellow student asked me whether I would like tickets for *The Magic Flute*. Yes, I said, if he had two! Shortly thereafter, L.L. arrived. I invited her to go to the opera and she accepted. Before we left, I asked Robert Weissman (in her presence) to please tell Bibring to bring his flour to dinner. (At the time, we were having the housekeeper in my building prepare us meals with food we brought in).

I was in a diabolical mood on the way to the opera. Despite the fact that we had had so much to say to each other over the last few weeks, I obstinately remained silent. She also said nothing, and the situation became uncomfortable. I kept thinking: You must say something! Feelings of inferiority began to rear their heads like filthy snakes, and I made some stupid remark about psychoanalysis. Her reply: "You really don't seem to be able to talk about anything else!" I was silent; the schlemiel in me had begun his game!

During the performance, I was not listening—my eyes were rivetted on her, sitting to my right—and I discovered a new aspect of her personality! Music! She sat hunched forward, and each lovely melody, especially Duhan's performance of Papageno, brought forth a naïve, childlike exclamation of delight. I saw only her laughing mouth, her shining eyes—I did not desire her as yet, for at the time she seemed such a child to me that just gazing at her filled me with joy! And then a sudden thought: What shall I say about the opera during the intermission? I shuddered, I knew very little about music, was aware of the fact that I had no opinion, and was afraid that . . . but what *was* I afraid of?

In the intermission, she introduced me to a gentleman with whom she conversed briefly. This man, she informed me, had written a book on ethics which she intended to give me. What was there to say: her friend had written a book on ethics!

We put on our coats and walked downstairs to the foyer, and I was looking forward to accompanying her home. Then, just before we reached the door, a figure came out of the shadows. I was introduced. Outside, he quite naturally slipped his arm in hers and headed off toward town. Momentarily, I felt as if someone had hit me on the head, and had only one thought: You are in love with her! The next instant, as I quickly said goodbye, I heard her call out, "I hope Bibring brought the flour!" I dashed off to the trolley stop, blinded by rage at her last remark and burning with love and jealousy.

What had happened? Why had she never mentioned him? Was he her boyfriend from Munich? The picture I had formed of her personality until then was irreconcilable with this last incident.

Everything within me was confused, agitated, and I was incapable of thinking! It was then that resentment first arose within me. It was very distant, something very foreign to me, hardly conscious; I feared that this had been her first lie—and I was later to be proven correct! The ridicule expressed in her concern about the flour was still ringing in my ears as I fell into a benumbed sleep.

The next day I was quieter, could no longer understand why I had been so disturbed the day before; nothing remained which even resembled jealousy or love, only bitterness over this kind of deceit.

I had turned in my final microscope slides and no longer came to the dissecting room—but I did see her with him twice, arm in arm, walking home down S.-strasse.

On December 18, I passed the anatomy examination with top grades. After the test, L.L. came to the examination room and presented me with a book by Jean Paul. She had inserted a card and written: "To good comradeship!" We exchanged only a few brief words; my relationship with her was the last thing on my mind. Later, when I came into the vestibule of the dissecting hall, she was standing there with a girlfriend and showed me a vase of orchids she had been given and a very beautiful engraved ring. I paid little attention to either and went on.

That afternoon, I met Robert Weissman, who informed me that Lia's birthday was the next day! Everything I had forgotten immediately came to life within me. I wanted to buy her a present, and my choice fell on *Mahler* by Specht. R.W. had drawn my notice to the book.

Nov. 29

I will not continue with this. What is the use? Yesterday Otto said that diaries were always written with the thought that they would someday be read. Let me be frank: I, too, have often entertained the thought that this should be (and would be) read, and yet the idea of someone reading it is—strange! Do I fear that I might be found out? Perhaps! What do I know of myself?

Otto's "Esoterik"*! Was it he who wrote this? How, amid the confusion of the age, did he arrive at these apodictic statements? "What does it matter to us that the goal is unreachable." Is that it? "To rest within oneself." All right! I would like to do that, too! But what if the outside world just happens to be against me? I cannot leave it, for I am dependent upon it! And Otto's second model: work! For whom? For myself? All right! But diaries are only written to be read. Therefore, there is still dependence upon the opinions of others! *Why does he write books and burn to see them published?* Is his ambition really so self-contained?

His girlfriend is Lisl—he loves her! She is affected, fairly intelligent, and what is she going to do? "Get married." Otto is blind and inconsiderate in his attitude toward young people, who he *thinks* are all just like himself! He asked her: "Do you want to make the acquaintance of Arabs who pay well?" "Yes." Out and out prostitution! Can it be categorized? I'm not bourgeois, but that's prostitution, no two ways about it!

But why shouldn't she be allowed to sell her body? That is the pivotal question! It is nobody's business—but to assist her in this? Where does that leave direction, conviction?

I also want to give "Esoterik" a closer reading!

Concerning "Esoterik":

About the epigraph: "View the facts with firmness and clarity. Anything that cannot live up to such scrutiny is . . . deceit!"

All right! The fact is: *Lore is dead.* I view this with firmness and clarity, and I see: (*a*) That she no longer knows anything, she has not lost anything! Only death itself is horrible! (*b*) That I am alone and face a summer without Lore, that I did not realize last year how much she meant to me. All "mourning" is egotistical! I am not mourning; yesterday I went to a concert, in the evening I walked arm in arm with Lisl for an hour and a half, deep in thought. I did not want to talk about Lore—not

---

*A paper by Otto Fenichel, written in 1918. [Eds.]

to Lisl! Lore's death is becoming a symbol for me. I am egotistical, after all! I view Lore's death with firmness and clarity!

Letter to Lore's uncle:

Nov. 30, 1920

Dear Sir:

*First I must ask you to excuse the fact that I am writing,
contrary to convention, in pencil—and now let me proceed immediately to the matter in hand.*

*Today at noon Mrs. Kahn visited me at the hospital in a
frenetic state. Indirectly, she accused me of stealing Lore's books
and presented a host of new ideas to support her theory about
an "operation." Aside from the effect of these accusations upon
me, I was plainly shocked by the condition of Lore's mother,
for I momentarily thought I had a case of paranoia before me.
A colleague who was present, and, incidentally, also knows Mrs.
Kahn, confirmed my fears. I tried to quiet her and promised to
visit her in the afternoon.*

*What struck me immediately was that the fabrication of these
and other similar ideas directed against me had begun only several days after Lore's death. This afternoon I paid her a visit
and easily succeeded in settling the matter of the books; but her
idea about an "operation," and the full extent of its absurdity,
was somewhat more difficult to clarify. My search for the origin
of the notion was futile, but after prolonged pressure she did
mention a doctor, although without disclosing his name. Shortly
thereafter, I discovered that you and your honorable brother, if
not the originators of the idea, had nevertheless promoted it. I
do not have the privilege of knowing you well, but I was aware
from the very beginning that you were not particularly fond of
me. As a matter of fact, I later discovered that you considered
me a rascal, a seducer "who had driven a girl to her death
through an 'operation.'" I should now like to state with all
firmness that I care little about your opinion of me and that this
letter is by no means to be construed as an explanation. It would*

perhaps not be superfluous to mention the fact that our own outlooks differ in every respect and to such a degree that any attempt to promote understanding would surely fail miserably. Just one thing: Lore was closer to me spiritually than to any member of her family and was a hundred times more intelligent and hardworking, and above all more decent *than all of your novices put together, in spite of "everything"!*

I was perfectly frank with Mrs. Kahn and beseeched her, in anticipation of what might happen, not to allow rumors to circulate about Lore. She did not follow my advice and Lore's reputation has "naturally" already been defiled. After all, how could it be otherwise? Once again, it gave "society" something to talk about!

Fantasy has been given free reign: seduction, an "operation," a tragic death—just like a cheap novel! This, however, would also be of little importance were it not known that in the majority of cases, among those who contribute to the filth of such social games, the fantasy becomes an accepted reality.* But this time I want to deprive them of all their satisfaction: this time it was not reality (it doesn't matter in the least whether or not anyone believes this).

One last comment: I feel that it is irresponsible, dangerous, and criminal if—in this case—you plant such ideas in the mind of Lore's mother or even so much as nourish them. Today, and over the course of the last few days, I have succeeded, through prolonged discussions which were ghastly for both parties, in proving the absurdity of these notions. I request that both you and your esteemed brother desist from these efforts if you do not wish to drive your sister insane. *Nor would I have written this* had I not seen the great danger so clearly today. *It is extremely serious!*

With hopes that you will recognize the justification of this request, and with the additional request that you not show this

---

*In an American biography of Reich published in 1983, this fantasy was presented as fact. [Eds.]

letter to Mrs. Kahn (to whom, incidentally, I have communicated its content), I remain,

> *Very truly yours,*
> *Wilhelm Reich*

What good is all the esotericism? Look at the letter and everything that led up to it. Lore dies; her mother, who has been in love with me for a long time, views me (perhaps!) as a substitute, showers me with kindness, addresses me as *"Du,"* kisses me, complains about her own marriage, and tells me that it soothes her to know that Lore had been happy at least for a short time, offers me Lore's room—I decline. Her self-accusations were then followed by attempts to brand me the murderer (literally!) of her daughter.* I fought against her and was barely able to control myself. Just as I succeeded in convincing her—hello! all the relatives arrive on the scene, claiming that I am a thief and a parasite, yes, even a murderer! My presentiments when I asked her not to publicize the affair, the feeling I had of choking on every bite I ate there—it has all come true! The inevitable consequences followed for one poor wretch. How Lore laughed at me when I was furious with myself the first time for having eaten fourteen instead of ten of her dumplings, how she called me insane when I told her I would visit her once every ten days instead of four times a week if it weren't for the invitations to dinner which I couldn't turn down. Lore, I myself, our love, and everything that was, and remained, beautiful in my memory has been defiled! Esotericism!

There is (and always will be) an unbridgeable gap between the "haves" and the "have-nots" who dare to complain of their fate and are vulgar enough to profit from their misery in at least one sense; namely, masochistic satisfaction! Disgusting! Esoter-

---

*[Added in 1937] As Lore still grappled with death, her mother found some bloody underclothes in a closet, apparently from a menstrual period long forgotten. She thought that Lore had carried out a "forbidden interference" (abortion) and had become fatally ill.

icism! Take a look, you who preach esotericism—go and try the life of a "have-not" yourself!

All your sympathetic "perception," all your empathizing cannot compensate for one minute of dismal brooding born of real distress. Of what use is all the esotericism; let's have practical action! When I am "favored" with an invitation to a rich man's home, all the esotericism in the world will not remove my justified feeling of being pitied, of receiving alms!

No esotericism will show me why Lore had to die, what drove me to run to the box office five days after her burial and buy up all concerts for the next three months, to storm into Manz's the same day and buy four hundred kronen worth of nonsensical books, and then ride out to see my relatives, and finally, despite my disinclination and contrary to my own resolution, to visit Lore's room, to take an hour's walk arm in arm with Lisl two days later and talk of unimportant matters, etc., etc., etc.

Now look how far I have come with that epigraph!

Dec. 3

Marie was buried today—and I felt love for Uncle Arnold!

I cried on the way to the grave—not for her, but because I had recollections of Mother's and Father's deaths. And then, too, I was alone, had found a fine girl—and she had to die, which left me alone again! Sabinski had to be killed in action, because he was my only childhood friend! I cause unhappiness. Nonsense, narcissism in its negative form!

In an hour Lore's mother is coming to visit me. I was very hateful to her yesterday and then felt so sorry immediately after leaving that I went back and left a note on her door! Why, after all, did she have to say that she had come to see me to tell me I was Lore's murderer! Yesterday she again had ideas about an "operation." I couldn't stand it anymore! The day before, I had conclusively accounted for every minute Lore had spent with me at the seminar, the concert, and at Grinzing* on Saturday and

*A pretty village now incorporated as a suburb of Vienna. [Eds.]

on Sunday (until twelve o'clock). I thought I would lose my mind! This is the hysterical comedy of a woman in menopause who has identified with her daughter and is lustfully wallowing in the idea of an "operation" despite its obvious absurdity. This wallowing is the hysterical symptom of a desire for an operation she really wanted—from me! That is as clear as day! If I do not see her for a day, then she pays me a visit for some trivial reason, kisses me, comes to my room, and says she should never have allowed Lore to undergo analysis; it offered too many good opportunities, although she realizes that months lay between Lore's analysis and our first date. She gives me meals, closes the door, removes the key, and when I want to leave, she tells me how her husband had thought it "improper" when she had once spoken with me in a darkened room. And the looks she gives me! They speak louder than words. What can be done here? Today I am to accompany her to the doctor who supposedly told her about the operation! I am certain that she will find a way to avoid going. I will make one last attempt and show her Lore's final diary entry, dated October 27 (four days before her illness), where she wrote: "Only one thing: a child!" If that doesn't help, then nothing will!

I feel so sorry for her!* She complains to me about how miserable her marriage is, a marriage which she entered into without love; she mentioned it in the first days after Lore's death, she envies Lore for the happiness she found at least for a short while—poor Lore! I always envision her with her hair down, as she was in Unterach, Geisshübl, on the Leopoldsberg—oh, those sublime nights! Out of doors, on a dewy meadow, the threads

---

*[Added in 1937] When later I was blamed for brutal thoughtlessness, the accusation was mistaken: not brutality, but inner softness was my greatest mistake. Indeed, I have often been forced in life to brutally overcome the result of this softness, which I am still fighting. I would like to warn my friends and pupils against it. It misleads me in situations which are unendurable or become so. The subsequent correction costs much more than if I had been firm at the start. Perhaps this softness, which some people call "hyperkindness" and "hypertolerance," is a defense against a very deep-seated and powerful ruthlessness. I wish I could rid myself of it in certain situations.

of mist danced around us like ghosts; below the Wien valley, with its forests shimmering blue in the moonlight; the stars, the sky—and she lying naked in my arms, her loosened hair tumbling down, my head upon her bare, white, soft breasts, blissful, perfectly satisfied (I had even forgotten the whore [Lia]) with Lore, my mistress and mother. "I have never been as happy as I am with you, my father and lover!" she would say, and her soft, gently trembling lips kissed my mouth and eyes! Lore, Lore. "How can you possibly love a person like me, ill-humored scoundrel that I am?" I asked her, remembering the whore. "I do not know, but I do love you!" and she embraced me more tightly. "Do you remember that night in Unterach?" "Yes, with you, yes, yes—!" "Oh, I was so afraid of you then and yet I loved you so—!" And our bodies came together intimately, lips upon lips, her hair tumbled over my head, all my yearning was fulfilled—I was content!! Lore!

Will there ever again be anything as beautiful as that young sun which awakened us in the morning? We shivered and wrapped ourselves tightly in shawls and blankets, forgot the people going out into their fields, forgot the world, the town—were one in body and soul!

I loathe that whore who would not let me find peace, who sought me out at 10 p.m., after I had been with Lore, and said, at 11:30 p.m., "I don't want you to have to go with me, but I'm afraid of walking alone!" Afraid, was she? The park, the night, the desire, the kisses. And the next day I went to visit her: Hans was also there and slapped her on the behind! In my presence! I am disgusted by that woman, whom, at the time, I wanted to possess only to prove to myself that I could have her, too, in full knowledge that it would all be over after the second time!

In my torment I fled to Lore—and she knew and understood all! One night we had all been to a concert and were on our way home. Lia and I were walking ahead, arm in arm, while Hans, his sister, Lore, and three other young people followed. Lia remarked, "Why are you doing this to Lore when you can't belong to her completely?" And I wanted to scream with rage, for I loved Lore at the same time that I ardently desired Lia's lithe body. That was the only time Lore made any mention of it: "I will tolerate your activities," she said, "until they are simply too ridiculous for me!" "You are right, Lore, but help me to get out of this!" She made no reply. When I did not see Lia for a time, I forgot everything, did not think about her anymore, and was at peace! I suffered dreadfully when, after seeing her again at a concert or a visit, I desired her and had to admit that I was being a scoundrel to Lore. I am not—will not be—polygamous! I also told Lore that before we went on our hike, whereupon she showed me a postcard from Frank and complained of being in the same situation. She had succeeded earlier than I in extricating herself! I was together with Lore in complete freedom only three weeks before the onset of her illness. How horrible it was at concerts when I did not wish to sit next to the one or the other—I could never really enjoy myself. Only once, when I attended a concert all by myself! And what disturbed my last bit of peace? A woman who was incapable of love, whose opinions and outlook were far less independent than Lore's. The woman was serious only where she had learned to be and I desired her only because a year before I had begun imagining her as my wife. I idealized her out of all proportion and would not allow myself to realize how shocked I was when I saw the truth!

Dec. 5

Sunday afternoon, three o'clock, it is cold in my room and I am all alone. In the morning I was at Mrs. Kahn's. She lied about the doctor having made a statement—I went to see him with her—she said she had "needed the white lie in order to prove me guilty." The whole thing was unbelievable; I wanted to go home but she insisted that I ride with her. I asked her whether she still believed it. "No!" she replied. Was pleased about that and spent several pleasant hours with her; she was calm. At noon the next day, she was still in bed, laid her cheek on my hand, and asked, "Didn't you go and fetch the instruments at the time?" She must see Schilder,* I said. Yes, she was willing to go, just to find peace. At 9 p.m. I spoke with Schilder after his lecture; she is to see him this afternoon at 4:30. Will she really go? Her brother was with her.

I have played my hand; there is nothing more for me to do in that family! Old people will never understand us!

I have become incapable of work, am unable to proofread a finished manuscript, have lost all desire and courage. My paper "Concerning the Energy of Drives"† is with Freud—he will surely shake his head and hand it back.

I am learning English—want to get away from Europe—but also want clinical psychiatry! First one, then the other! Will it fly? If I could only work! I feel that I am going downhill! What a difference in the amount of energy I have now, compared to two years ago. My ambition has been extinguished, flares up only on rare occasions. Have I acted correctly? If I had not destroyed my ambition, it might have drowned out everything else.

I am back to zero again!

Dec. 10

The last act of the tragedy: Lore's mother committed suicide by gassing herself. Discovered this today by chance through Moser!

There is no way to avoid the feeling that I am the murderer of an entire family, for the fact remains that if I had not entered that household, both of them would still be alive! And with this on my mind I continue my life—more lectures, analysis, concerts. I am acting out a comedy, while causing the people around me

*Paul Ferdinand Schilder, M.D. (1886–1940)—Professor of Psychiatry at the University of Vienna. Interested in bridging the gap between the organic and the functional. [Eds.]
†Published in *Zeitschrift für Sexualwissenschaft*, Vol. 10, 1923. This article is included in Reich's *Early Writings, Volume One* (New York: Farrar, Straus and Giroux, 1975). [Eds.]

to die! Didn't my own mother also die—better said, also commit suicide—because *I* had told all? I seek relief from this heavy burden; who will help me? Who am I and what can I do? Why do I bring about such tragedies of life and death?

I wanted her to see Schilder, but she wouldn't go. And then she killed herself, two days after I had written her, saying, "You will understand that I cannot visit you for some time." What should I have done—or not done? Should I not have loved Lore?

How infinitely sad it all is!

Poor Willy!* I wonder why he didn't contact me?

What am I now to that whole family? I cried for Lore, who belonged to me; I didn't care about anyone else!

But this time it's different, for I am the cause—not a soul to help me! It's awful! Who will tell me how I should have behaved? I was the cause, but could I have helped it? Who will tell me what I am?

Dec. 24

A pure, simple joy: my analysand brought me two packs of Egyptian cigarettes as a Christmas present! He left analysis prematurely without being cured, and yet he presented this token!

Otto held his reading,† two full evenings! An almost completely synthetic self-criticism—his attitude toward communism is not clear, long-winded comments on nationalism which were directed against me.

Shall I answer in writing as I have already done in words? Perhaps it will crystallize in time!

Lisl is a clever girl when she is not affected, and I think her prostitution is a reaction formation.

Bibring is set on psychiatry! We have a good understanding. Has he changed, or have I? No, both of us have!

Today, that Geisha Osen‡ riled me up again! I want it to be

---

*Willy Kahn—Lore's brother. [Eds.]
†"On Founding a Commune in Berlin—1921/22." [Eds.]
‡Osen—a writer of romantic literature. [Eds.]

summertime and have a woman! Don't bother me with philosophy!

Dec. 27

Two weeks ago, I had my first obstetric duty and felt a sense of satisfaction about the work because I had really learned a great deal in just a few days. The mothers, and especially the newborn children, with whom I played during every spare minute I had, gave me such joy.

Jan. 1, 1921

New Year's Eve at Lia's. It was beautiful, wonderful! Read from Strindberg, Kraus, and Werfel—then a night of abstinence! We will always find each other somehow. It really was a beautiful night! I felt no inhibitions, spoke of Lore—and met with understanding.

Jan. 3

Robert left for Bucharest today. Suddenly I felt very sad! There is so little understanding between us, and yet I like him! I wish him much, much happiness!

I have put things in order; a lot of junk—more than a lot—was thrown out!

Bought 560 kronen worth of books at Manz's. Granted, they are beautiful—but how frivolous of me! Something within me sought abreaction! I suddenly felt so lonely, so entirely alone, as I walked home through the streets of the inner city after saying goodbye to Robert! What if I never see him again? I was still unable to resolve those infantile death wishes. My unconscious is full of horrible hatred toward him!

A picture of Lia is before me. How is it that for weeks I feel no yearning for her and then . . . At any rate, it seems strange: every few weeks, a night of abstinence!

I want love—I want a woman!

How bourgeois I am! A commune? I would enjoy going to

Berlin! But a commune? Perhaps—with people whose life patterns somehow match my own. Otto? Lia? Preferably Otto! Lia? Rather with Lore than anyone else! She was the only person who would have fit into a commune! Not I, Lia, or Otto!

Damn! Why am I now experiencing this fear of being alone! When I bought those beautiful books, the thought of having a lovely summer was constantly in the back of my mind—but with whom?

Lore is dead! How that sounds: dead! *Dead!* Death and life! What is death and why do we live? It is easy for people who don't think about it. I am alive, have two *paying* patients sent to me by Freud himself! And there will be more coming—and then? I will write monographs and reports—very good ones at that, naturally! And then? If the situation with the working man weren't so dismal! Politics, oh, politics!

Is there any possible way to arrange a life with human beings which includes both the greatest possible accomplishment and the most sublime pleasure?

Attended a concert yesterday—the Rosé Quartet: Brahms, and a quintet by Schubert. I heard nothing, for I was in a dream.

I was off in a cloud and dreamed such a wonderful, wonderful dream: The Kahlenberg—at night—the brightest silvery moonlight flowed over delicate wisps of mist covering the valley at Krapfenwald, which, enveloped in a dark backdrop to the right, opens out to the left—on the Danube, spanned by bridges where only a row of lights could be seen and then, more and more distinct, the grand city in its vague shimmer—peace, peace—*Andante un poco adagio* . . .

"Wouldst thou guide me, lead me through the peaceful night? Come, my darling, show me life and I shall show you pleasure in return!"

A tall girl, with long, flowing hair, in a loose garment, spoke from a sweet little mouth; I kissed her hand, leaned against her—shoulder to shoulder, cheek to cheek—and far beyond,

beyond the gray-gold city, the sky opened up. Two large, bony hands wave—you call out—why should that not be possible?

No! Joyous, calling, singing—Leopoldsberg—the church rising from the old wall—below us the deep Danube valley—clothes off, and we danced, naked as our mothers bore us, danced, danced, so close to the edge.

Scherzo (Allegro)—we danced, danced, naked as the children of God, in the long shadows of our bodies cast by a silent moon—peace drew us together again and I buried my heated brow in her tender thighs, covered my head with her long blond hair—so close to the edge—while we wound our arms around and around each other like serpents and my brow found her soft white breast.

Oh, what a pitiable psychoanalyst I am! How well I know what all this means!

Jan. 11

No work on Sunday. Nobody should work on Sunday—I decided to try something different. From two to three in the afternoon, I had an analytic session with a patient who was unable to come on Monday. At 3:30 there was the Rosé Quartet; I did not attend, for I didn't have a ticket—although I could have gotten in. I had already put my coat on—but no! I shall do some studying! English! Then the Jewish castration complex! I want to speak on this subject the next time there is a lecture evening at the Psychoanalytic Society! But to what purpose?

At four o'clock I called Lia to ask her to come at seven and translate an English monograph. She had gone to the concert, so I left word. At six o'clock I went to the cafeteria. Then tried to read Adler. He is interesting but wrong! Attempted to read Strindberg—quarter to seven—will she come? I built a fire in the stove—seven-thirty—called again, couldn't get through, well then, to hell with it! Wrote a letter to Lisl, and to Grandmother. Read Strindberg—*Inferno*—more and more Strindberg,* i.e., reading about myself, smoking, reading, thinking—there was a high-pitched whistle from the iron stove I am so proud of, the long lament of the wind—I am reading *Inferno*, Robert is in Rumania, Lore is lying out there, all decomposed; Bibring is with his relatives. Shall I write the story of my life from Mother's death to Father's? Sadger wants to have it published; it will supposedly yield a ten percent royalty: Hooray!

You can't get any work done on Sunday . . .

THE CUTAWAY

Ten dollars arrived from America! A quick look to find the exchange rate: 6,580 kronen, but half belongs to Robert! Hm! 3,290 kronen is next to nothing! He owes me more than that, anyway.

Bibring and I in a fabric shop. I found a dark-gray material for a two-piece suit. Good! Bibring: "You should have striped pants and a cutaway!" I was taken aback! A cutaway? For what? When will I ever wear a cutaway?

It's something you can always use! "Look," he said, "just the other day Fritz Lehner invited all his friends over. Everyone appeared in a cutaway, and I happened to be wearing one myself!" "Hm! Lehner! But shall I ever be invited to Lehner's? Fool! No, I will never wear a cutaway coat!" Bibring: "As you wish! I can only give you my advice!" What do you say, Mr. X.? A two-piece suit or a cutaway? Whatever you prefer, sir! A cutaway is more elegant! Aha! More elegant! But, oh, dear—white acces-

---

*[Added in 1937] I was sick with excitement when I read Strindberg. He appeared to have experienced in its essence the problem of mutual matrimonial compulsion. I knew he had not solved this problem, but his *To Damascus* and *Confession of a Fool*, and similar masterpieces, revolutionized me fundamentally. I had lived with the feeling that my parents' catastrophe was a terrible exception to the rule of peaceful union between man and woman. The Viennese bourgeoisie gave the outward appearance of idle happiness. But why did everybody forsake Strindberg and philosophize about morals and sexual faithfulness? Why did this concern them more than the misery of daily life that I partook of?

sories: a hat, shoes! Bibring: "And besides, you can have a suit made the next time money arrives from America! But the cutaway you need now: think of graduation!" "I don't give a damn." Bibring: "Don't put on such an act. You'll be a doctor, and after that there will be one occasion after the next . . . !" I could already see my tails flapping! "Is it proper to wear a cutaway without a hat? In the summer?! I don't have a hat! That would be one more problem!" Bibring: "Just don't worry about that!"

All right, a cutaway, please! 2.1 meters of black material for the coat and 1.1 for the striped trousers! There! Now I'm "fit for the Lehners." 5,170 kronen, please pay at the desk! I have a queasy feeling. Something is not right! "How much does one need for a regular suit?" 2.8 meters. "Am I going to sacrifice 30 centimeters (= 500 kronen) for this foolishness?" "It doesn't make any difference. You need a cutaway, and I'm happy that you are having one made!"

Next I went to the tailor's. A cutaway or a regular coat? A cutaway is more elegant. Hm! He must know! My fee for a cutaway is a hundred kronen more. Well, if it really is more elegant! Stylish! Ha! So I'm getting a cutaway!

But one question is still bothering me: where and in what company will I wear it? Wait! Bibring said at weddings and dress balls. Weddings? My cousins (both male and female) have already found their spouses, thank God! No prospects there. Dress balls? There is still that possibility. Well, perhaps. We shall see!

But I don't go to dress balls! "Of course you'll go! It's unwholesome to close oneself off from the world!" That is what Bibring said, and I guess if he says so . . .

It was on Monday and Tuesday that a cutaway was decided upon for me!

On Thursday there was a performance of *Flamme* in the Volkstheater. I lined up for standing room (picturing myself in a cutaway). Only one side of the double doors was opened and we were being shoved to the ticket window like swine, girls and women were screaming, at the next entrance tickets were being sold at black-market prices for two hundred kronen. I shouted to the usher: "You really could have opened both sides of that door!" At that, two policemen pushed me back into line, not exactly gently, and barked, "That's none of your business. Your business is to stay in line!" "I'll speak when I please!" (I am already in an uproar inside.) And I repeat: "You really could have opened both sides of that door so we don't get pushed around like pigs!" "Don't you go making any rules! Understand? Otherwise, we'll show you out! That's right, you'll be shown out!" I was somewhat quieter. "I'm sure you wouldn't resort to that! And don't you push people around, mister!" I had called a policeman "mister"—well, that peeved him.

I got a place up front, just behind the rail, and laid my hat on the floor in the aisle where the ladies and gentlemen would soon begin to file past.

Oh, the women! Clothed but exposed! Gentlemen in tuxedos; ha, there is a cutaway, and another! A bureaucrat, for sure! That is how I will look! Another cutaway with his lady, a fat slob (I beg your pardon); stupid women, fleshy; earrings, tuxedos, patent-leather ankle boots; the curtain has gone up, the tuxedos keep coming and are disturbing the people who have standing room in the orchestra! I am furious, can't these barbarians arrive on time? I bark at one of the tuxedos (or was it a cutaway?) to stop where he is. He keeps on walking.

The ticket taker places himself in front of a haughty couple —tuxedo and bare shoulders—and they walk right past him. A gray coat and a girl in a simple dress are not allowed through.

Flamme is a bad story by Hans Müller about a prostitute. No, I will not wear a cutaway. Went to the tailor's, luckily he had not yet begun; I was pleased and enormously proud of myself!

Jan. 12

A dream: I hear someone saying, "Rashly turning, rashly turning!" Otto, Edi Bibring, and my brother are sitting at a table. I say to Bibring with a laugh, "How fine it would be if the analyst had a key to his unconscious, could open it during each analysis and then close it again!" We laughed. In saying this, I made a gesture of turning a key with my right hand.

I ask my brother, with whom I am now alone, how he is doing at his new job. "Bad," is his reply. I am amazed that he is sitting there with the rest of us.

I vaguely recall a girl I met on a journey under peculiar circumstances.

I awoke after the dream and tried to interpret it while I was still half asleep. The words "Rashly turning," which I had heard someone call out so clearly, immediately caught my attention. They stem from my studying English, the story about a man who "turns rashly" (in a windy place). It also has to do with Hamlet's father, who wanders about as a ghost. Mysticism. On the evening of the dream, I was reading Strindberg's *Inferno* and had noticed the man's paranoid traits after the separation from his wife. Through this, as well as through his predilection for moneymaking, I became acquainted with his homosexuality for the first time. I am reading the book with great interest. That same evening there had been a reading of Freud (*Infantile Neurosis*) at Otto's, as always on Tuesdays. We discussed the difficulties of analytic technique and each of us contributed his own experiences. Among other things, I remarked that, on the basis of three cases, I had been convinced that homosexuality, which is normally subjected to far greater repression than heterosexuality, might well also play the greater role in the etiology of neurosis.

Jan. 13

It is becoming increasingly obvious that I am analyzing Annie Pink with intentions of later winning her for myself—as was the case with Lore. She flees from men; I am supposed to enable her to release her drives and at the same time to become their first object. How do I feel about that? What must I do? Terminate the analysis? No, because afterwards there would be no contact!

But she—what if she remains fixated on me, as Lore did? Resolve the transference thoroughly! Yes, but is transference not love, or, better said, isn't all love a transference?

A young man in his twenties should not treat female patients.

Jan. 14

Lisl Brauner, a prostitute because of an inner compulsion, with whom I wanted to have intercourse. While I am kissing her, she is calculating, refuses me. It is unpleasant for me, for I cannot believe that this is her genuine attitude. I spoke with her about it yesterday and soon saw a different person before me. How horrible! She was seduced by her father, has developed a fixation on him, and submits to all the other men because she can't have him. (Annie Pink has a father and brother fixation, but she flees from all men.) She has never had a boyfriend to understand or help her. Her father-image is that of an unintelligent man. She cried so hard, was so entirely different—my very first efforts produced a collapse of the normal superstructure and I was faced with an intelligent, unhappy, eighteen-year-old girl who had been seduced by her father and loves her body, although she gives it to men she does not care about or even like. I must not tell her that I want to help her; otherwise, everything will be lost. I see her now in a different way. She poured out her heart until one in the morning and stayed overnight with me; naturally, we did not think of having intercourse. I lay down on the chaise longue half dressed, for she had to leave very early, before my landlady awoke. I dozed off, then heard her cough—once, twice. I imagined that she had called to me—I resisted this. Attempted to fall asleep again, for I did not want her to belong to me that night and knew that she could not. Then the thought came: Won't she consider you an impotent fool? One voice answered: Nonsense! While something else drove me to get up. I went to her bed—she was asleep. I kissed her hair softly. She awoke, held out her arms, and kissed me. I was brash enough to consider this reason to slip into her bed. But she began to cry; I was desperate, for I did not want it to happen.

"You are no better than all the rest!" "Thank you, Lisl! You are entirely right!" And not ashamed, but once again *myself*, I went back and fell into a deep, peaceful sleep.

In the morning, after I had accompanied her downstairs and opened the door, she remarked, "Willy Reich, all night long I dreamed that you were getting into bed with me!"

Poor Lisl! In the end, she is more decent than all of us together! You just have to be able to see, and want to see! I like her!

[No date]

A restaurant on the outskirts of the city. Across from me at a small table sit He and She huddled together before a bottle of white wine. She is spreading butter on a piece of bread while he talks to her. He leaves the restaurant for a moment. She remains quietly seated; soon she glances at the corner to my right as if her eyes had been drawn by a magnet, but only for a second; then she grows uneasy, looks for some way to busy herself, takes out a handkerchief, straightens her blouse, her hair, looks over again, a quick but clear nod of her head. He comes back in; they sit nestled close together, whispering intensely . . .

Jan. 17

Concert: Mahler's *Klagende Lied*! Lia, Hans Swarowski, Annie Hartl, and others.

Hans Swarowski is already wearing communist insignia! I walked Annie Hartl home. There was a park along the way— oh, why did I kiss her? What a really pitiful soul I am! Bernfeld, she said, spoke poorly of me; what does he know about me, and where did he get his information? Everybody dislikes me! If someone could only tell me what causes people who have neither met nor spoken with me to have a negative opinion. Not that I care—or do I? No, not as a rule, but perhaps when it is Siegfried Bernfeld, I do! I must ask Otto! He once disliked me, too!

What could be the reason? Annie Hartl found me crude! Correct, that I am; crude and inconsiderate, and I take even *this* to extremes! Annie Pink told her that she didn't want to be analyzed by someone reckless!

Oh, well, so what!

Jan. 24

The discussion of "*Peer Gynt*" in the Psychoanalytic Society was an extreme blow to my faith, a blow which I experienced all the more acutely due to my injured narcissism. They were not opponents but doubters! Now that I have begun to *think*, I discover that another person might have arrived at essentially different results. "Is there an unconscious?" I asked Otto. His reply: "In a psychoanalytic sense, yes; in a philosophical sense, no!"

There are Fröschels* and there are Hitschmanns! The first group reasons that since the assumption of an unconscious is not philosophically deducible, it does not exist; thus, Freud is incorrect. The second group says: Let us not philosophize, but analyze, analyze; ana—ana—anal!

How shall I find my way through? Fröschels, Hitschmanns! Ideas actually emerge of which I knew nothing beforehand; therefore, there must be an unconscious!

But these new ideas are only perceivable after they emerge. I postulate an unconscious.

Feb. 2

When I think how complicated, inflated, and pompous the entries in my diary are, I feel ashamed—and very much so! And yet there was an element of truth in those emotions. I cannot decide how much has been taken over from others—or about taking-over in general! If I enjoy music so much today, if music captivates me so completely, despite my relationship with Lia Laszky, who introduced me to it in Vienna, then there must be

---

*Fröschel—a philosophically oriented physician who doubted the existence of completely unconscious psychic images. [Eds.]

something within me that was merely awakened at that time! How different it was with her and psychoanalysis: she fell in love with me and bought Freud's writings, was interested in them, sometimes even enthusiastic, and then . . .

Feb. 6
(During the analysis of Annie Pink) It is awful when a young, pretty, intelligent, eighteen-year-old girl tells a twenty-four-year-old analyst that she has long been entertaining the forbidden idea that she might possibly embark on an intimate friendship with him—yes, that she actually wishes it, says it would be beautiful—and the analyst has to resolve it all by pointing to her father.

Feb. 10
Annie Pink pays fifty kronen per analytic session. It is getting better for her and easier for me! All compulsion and alienation have been eliminated (I think she will read this someday!). Whence my aversion to accepting her money? Is an analyst permitted to enter into a relationship with a female patient after a successful analysis? Why not, if *I* desire it!

Feb. 27
How peculiar it is to reread things written in the past! Sounds so strange, neurotic! Annie Pink means no more to me than any other patient—Lore was behind that, just as Annie continually identifies with Lore—basta!

Much has happened—actually, with very little said; very quietly and peacefully, a lot has changed. Otto, Bibring, Grete Lehner, Lisl Brauner.

Otto is a pigeonhole person, puts everyone in a particular slot: "Catalogue X will be visiting me on Friday night!" Horrible! I really like Otto; he is extremely fond of me, too. I'm sure I'm high on his list, but then, what good does it do me?

Grete Lehner is revolutionizing but—just for fun. And where does her seriousness begin?

Lisl Brauner: intelligent, clever, indolent, feline. She is searching for her father and will never find him.

How wonderful it was last night! Two primitives, naked on
the floor before the fire. Lisl is beautiful when she is naked, so
infinitely tender, with life in every fiber! No wonder she doesn't
want to find a job! And yet she must! She is so dreadfully lazy
—I think she is still very sick. What is a woman to do who does
not want to work, perhaps because she is so full of pleasure—
hey, Max Stirner! Bibring represents one aspect of my personality, and Lisl the other. In reality, I struggle with each one of
them about the standpoint of the other; to be truthful, though,
I am struggling with myself! I love Lisl and yet I don't—she isn't
motherly at all. I took her yesterday, she gave herself to me—
and then shed tears because she doesn't love me. Poor Lisl—
her father! It is better this way than if she loved me. Our minds
drew closer and our bodies followed, the body *must* be followed.
This morning it was so repulsive, we were both so horribly
oppressed!

I went for a hike alone, but was not at all refreshed when I
arrived home. I need a woman who is both mother and whore.

Somehow I am currently in a phase of stagnation despite the
fact that I do a lot of reading, studying, working, analyzing. I
think, and I fear that with me every forward thrust must be
preceded by restless, confusing, neurotic mental activity. I am
afraid of stagnation; i.e., Bibring. He is not in motion at all,
always stays the same, considers it a great "revolutionary" deed
to have obtained permission to go to a café in the evening (Lehner's) for the first time in two years—people have such strange
ideas! And how childishly and blindly he behaves in regard to
Grete Lehner's analysis. But what business is it of mine? And
yet I need two people: a man and a woman!

I think I will soon stop keeping a diary; it doesn't make sense
and it's childish. But there is one thing I would still like to do;
namely, somehow to compile all my developmental stages up to
now and write it down in a condensed form, systematically
classified. But for what?

Everything is filth! Live for the moment, oh man, and do not attempt to make others happy.

March 12

When bodies remain tumescent—I would never have believed it could happen! A dreamlike walk for an hour and a half through parks and past churches; yesterday I experienced a kiss for the first time! Wild little whore—Lisl—my child! Prolonged tumescence. She cannot be a mother to the man who has become a child after the final organ regression. After coitus the whore must become a mother, just as the polygamous man then becomes a monogamous child! If we could only remain in the first state and thus spare ourselves the repulsiveness of "the morning after"!

We prayed before the Karlskirche, whose massive form cut into the starry, blue-black heavens. "If only we were naked!"

"—and thus to stroll slowly, body touching body, very slowly, alone with our souls in a vast, infinite garden, on a carpet of soft green moss, beneath alder shrubs and tall trees with low-hanging branches, ever denser and finally so close that we are completely closed in, and yet we continue along, for the branches open before us and close when we've passed, body touching body. Do you see the rock, Lisl, the rock of uncertainty and the future—but let us continue, simply continue, for it *will* give way!"

The rock of the future?

Communist gibberish and egotistical reality! Look at Russia! Max Stirner, the god who saw in 1844 what we do not see today in 1921! Somehow I am growing increasingly secure in my conviction that a system of economic communism which lacks a candid acknowledgment of egotism is an impossibility. Man is egotistical not only in Adler's sense but also in matters of sex. *Altruism is only a form of egotism*, although it is of greater value than the purely subjective form of egotism. Can mankind be educated to this higher form? *No! Man cannot be educated at* *all! All education is a matter of transference as ecphorizational element!**

I don't want to be pompous! But let us come together to examine a question theoretically, my question! *For once*, let us do without rapture and ecstasy, for they impede prudent action when the outside world must be circumvented since it cannot be crushed! You have always placed much too much emphasis on the form which determined the content, and gushed over Kraus even when he drooled! But when you passed a beggar or a cripple who held out his hand, you wavered: to give or not? Admit it: every kind of decision became burdensome, for *giving* means helping, but it is also a cheap way to buy oneself freedom from giving even more, and therefore no better than the acts of those from whom you claim to differ. *Not giving* means being coldhearted, but it also implies respect for human dignity, which does not want to receive but prefers to take. Or you may remain consistent. Then you must not only speak but *also act*. So long as the last beggar has not vanished from our streets, the last woman in childbed gone without a noonday meal, the last louse sucked its last blood in a derelicts' night shelter, the last five-year-old crossed your path bent with a heavy load of wood so that he faces the ground and cannot see the sun, unwashed, hungry, his hands blue with cold as you wander off into the mountains on Sunday morning with your walking shoes and your full rucksack, delighted at your own intellectuality and closeness to nature, and indignantly turn your back on the bourgeoisie—so long as this goes on, I say, you may not (*if you are consistent*) buy books, frequent a summer resort, listen to music, go to the theater, have a midmorning snack or more than bread alone for supper, may not go on outings, not even study at the university, for your studies cost money and you are a heavy financial burden on some third party, no matter who it is—for you must live and if you are not earning, someone else

*Reich was influenced here by the work of Richard Semon. [Eds.]

must earn for you. And it makes no difference whether it is your uncle, your father, your aunt, or your lover who drains the workers' blood or whether you do it yourselves. Yes, I would even say that yours is the greater deceit, for the industrialist *admits* that he has enslaved a thousand people for his profits, even if he does attempt to justify it with "It has always been done this way," or "It is God's will," or some other excuse. And I will tell you outright that all your lamenting the "injustice" of the world does not impress me; I ignore it completely, for it is false, a lie, if it is not followed by action and resolution. And I am one of you, and all of us are like the others, and they in turn are just like those who extort, manipulate, solicit, steal, smuggle, coerce—we will all be "one of them" as long as there is one last person searching for bread in the middens!

Bear the consequences of your revolutionary spirit, if you can! Let someone stand up and say, "I will do it." That person will only be speaking empty words, or—if he follows through with actions—he will become a martyr and be no different from a cloistered ascetic, his previous archenemy, except that he is aware of acting out of egotism.

And if someone else should stand up and say, "We are honest and frank in our revolutionary sentiments, we are not egotists, but world capitalism and reaction are still too powerful, we cannot oppose them; resolute action is monstrous, we don't want to be martyrs—but only to help wherever we can!" Then I must ask: Can you help at all? Aren't you dependent yourselves? Granted, your support, as such, is assured, but are you not powerless beyond that? Do you want to help when you have become independent? We shall talk about that when the time comes. But one thing: let someone show me three members of the Youth Movement in all Vienna who grew up and also "grew up"! I hope you understand me! And even if you were willing, would you be able to prevail against a world full of enemies, for even your best friends are too egotistical not to be enemies in the final outcome! What you call a friend is merely a part of yourself in another person, but—mark my words—it is only a part, a sector of two overlapping life spheres! A very sad truth —but we must recognize it and therefore do better!

I reject the consequences of intellectual, revolutionary idiocy. Otto Kaus gives lectures on the materialist theory of history at the Volksbildungsheim [People's Education Center]; he and his wife are communists. Umansky is a consultant on the art of the Soviet Union in Vienna. After a lecture, Umansky asked Gina Kaus, who was wearing an elegant hat and a fur coat, to donate a coat for a Hungarian student who had fled to Vienna after the fall of the Räterepublik.* She admits to owning three coats, but unfortunately, for one reason or another, she was unable to make this donation! If at that time I was seized by a desire to spit on her, the reason was not her refusal to hand over a coat but rather the communist-altruist equality-liberty-and-fraternity postulated by the phony five-pointed star she wore!

The socialist and psychologist of the individual, Alfred Adler, sits in the Café Central night after night, a luminary to his gaping disciples, who listen as he ponders the problem of world socialism and rattles on about the struggle of feelings of community against the will to power, about socialist objectives, etc., and meanwhile a dance of death is going on outside. This would not concern us here if Adler were not mimicking an altruist!

Our god, Karl Kraus! A person—may it be said in this circle despite some knitting of brows—who bathes in applause and comes out to take a tenth bow on the platform, none of which I would criticize were he or his followers willing to admit that this is egotism in its crassest form and that his *Last Days of Mankind* is a product of narcissism, which as such, and in spite of it, has great parallel objective intellectual value!

March 13

Today I was in Mödling, Hinterbrühl, Anninger, Baden—alone. Lay in the sun for two hours, fell asleep and didn't recognize the mood I was in afterwards: for no reason, I was so

---

*A regime established after World War I. [Trans.]

happy, lighthearted, and cheerful, as I walked down that wonderful path through the woods to Baden. Not even the faintest
memory of last Saturday night. And that evening itself? Horrible
experiences which make one mature: (1) The death of all our
hopes for revolution, which the play demonstrated to me; (2)
Annie Pink, whom I accompanied home; (3) Lisl.

I am so dejected, do not want to write about these three
important issues at the moment; they are firmly rooted within
me anyway!

But one thing: after my mother committed adultery, my father
should have taken a hike *all by himself* in some beautiful, hilly,
wooded region. He would have seen everything differently!

March 23

Lore, the only representative of an unconditionally pleasure-
seeking type, appeared yesterday. I myself do not belong to this
type entirely. Lore tapped her feet on the ground and said, "Tap!
Tap! Here I am!"

Yes, she was here and exerted her influence and I grew healthy
through her (perhaps only after her death?). Helene Guttmann
and Lisl Brauner are the other type; I call them hysterical hyper-
sensualists.

Helene, Lisl, Lia are here—and in my heart.

Lore is out there—and in my heart.

Whores and mothers—but I will crush the whore within me!
Why does intellectuality include whoredom? How right Weininger was! But enough!

And the other! Otto wants to become an associate and then
a full professor—at least, that is his *wish.*

And I am so utterly alone!

Annie Pink is a fine woman, very neurotic, somehow like
Helene—but I think (and hope) the analysis is starting to take
effect. She is "disgusting" (her own expression) when she feels
inferior. She has nothing, must first "become"—but alone; she
must do it herself! Analysis is meant to serve this purpose. Do
I already love her? No! Or, rather, yes, the girl lying there with

her charming offers. The way she is today—no; the way I would like her to be—yes!

March 29

What is to be expected when one goes on a three-day Easter hike by oneself and meets a female patient in a meadow in an entirely unpopulated area—when one is not even certain whether it is really she, for one does not believe in such coincidences— when we are sitting across from each other in the inn the next day, when we continue the hike together and then again not together, down the same path but with a very big distance between us? I am beginning to wonder about my "firmness" during the treatment! She is extremely neurotic—but I think she could change.

It makes so little sense that I myself am the one who can never reach my goal despite my monogamous tendency (of course it's a lie), for I would be monogamous if I could find: the nimbleness and self-confidence of a Lia; the mind, intimacy, and whorishness as well as the naked beauty of a Lisl—to stimulate my own capabilities; the realness, the motherliness of a Lore for respite and support; and the possibility of having an outdoor hiking companion such as I find in Annie! All of this in one person . . .

March 31

Lisl is ill: hysteria! Hysterics should visit me only during my office hours. How stupidly I behaved toward her.

Why do I repeatedly plunge in head over heels and lose myself?! Well, this time I found myself again quickly—perhaps because I do not love her!

Today I felt it: my relatives are nonexistent, they are more alien to me than the lowliest chimney sweep in the Volkscafé! They are so stupid, narrow-minded, vain. Gossip, filth! Even the best of them—enough of that!

How is it possible? This question of whether my father was made of different stuff than I—or is there no such thing as heredity? Oh, what difference does it make, anyway!

A sad evening: unfulfillment weighs upon my soul, my body sits here on the fourth floor, my eyes gaze out into the square courtyard, while my nerves sense the springtime. Where is *my* girl? How old I am; how long will this searching go on? Alone with my thoughts, delving, stirring, yearning to shape a human being—to reach out—

It is all such a mess, summer after summer passes by, the summer of my life is near; death, the ghastly one, nears with the racing ticktock of the second hand . . .

Is it neurotic that I should want a woman, a woman of my own, for I cannot and will not be alone! To hell with all my activities, analytic, scientific, medical, and otherwise—if the irretrievable hours of youth are to slip by without a woman! I will start writing books when my mental and physical potency has evaporated in the arid wastelands of science! Spring tempests of human yearning—why must masochism be the fulfillment? Look at others: Edi and Grete! How can two people have each other and live together for two and a half years without possessing each other? How this throng of bodies jostles and shoves and dashes and runs after illusions, how it murders and rapes and ruins and does not see the present moment! And just what am I doing while I write this? What good is it, and for whom? Isn't there anything better, happier, more beautiful? A girl is sitting over there, fantasizing just as I am, and we do not see each other—do not know each other! Perhaps we will meet someday, and then there will be a family and filth and gossip! Oh, it is so sad!

And now, girl, fling your soft, bare arms around my neck so that I may kiss their gentle curves; remove your clothes so that I may have you naked—and likewise naked give myself to you. Our bodies' trembling shall be the measure of our souls' bliss —thus would I melt within you, fade away inside your body. I would forget the pain of my soul and savor eternal seconds between your soft thighs, inhale deeply the smell of your hair, of your body—

Oh, *sexus, sexus*—dominant of all existence!

This is so stupid, not even writing yields relief; I am not a poet and do not wish to be one, but I do want to live, and how dreadful that one cannot live alone.

April 4

The world and its people! Lia, that same Lia who wrote me such letters from 's Hertogenbosch has joined the clique in the Café Central!

May 2

Together with B.B.*—the Wachau†—Otto. Annie was so incredibly dear today! If she only knew!

Why am I so annoyed at hearing that Otto went off somewhere yesterday at noon, probably with Berta. Do I love her? No! Am I in love with her? No! I simply feel very loving toward her, and that is something entirely different!

On returning home, I was not more peaceful, but rather more confused, agitated, saw things less clearly. For a long time I have had fantasies of being together with Annie—*a child of ours would certainly be very beautiful and intelligent*! On the ride back, I repeatedly envisioned her after the birth of a child—and both of us standing by the cradle!

What is Annie? (I hardly know what to write!) Pretty? Yes! And well built! Clever? Certainly, very! Somewhat narrow horizons. Can she be loving? I doubt it! She is one of those women who want only to *be* loved. Maybe! Why am I thinking so seriously of marrying her? What can I be for her, what can she be for me? One thing I know: I could love her very, very much! But she would require something more than what she has now, and above all, there would have to be a remission of the neurosis!

Alas, in the end, one always remains alone!

---

*Berta Bornstein—a psychoanalyst. [Eds.]
†A picturesque region along the Danube. [Trans.]

June 1

I am in it up to my ears again, the whole mess! I'm feeling sour—it was this way last year when I was yearning for a woman—and I have sleeping sickness, I sleep at the microscope, while diagnosing, analyzing, writing—I just fall asleep.

I do not love Annie yet, but the great danger lies in the fact that when I do begin to love and desire her, it will not be easy to extricate myself. I am still on my guard, for the more likely it seems that we are compatible, the greater the caution required. And she does not suit me—nonsense, she is an eligible woman. But I am not yet sure just how to broach matters.

Oh, this artifice! Why are we not allowed to attain our happiness through that simple and beautiful means: understanding. She would have to leave a lot behind; above all, her blind pursuit of ideals and her idiotic search for authority!

Lisl—who suddenly wanted to be alone and left us! How laughable! Those hunched-up shoulders of hers and her wobbly head—a mouth which has lost track of the brain!

If I were only allowed to take Annie's face in my hands, give her a hearty, healthy kiss on the lips, and say, "Let's give it a try!"

But, alas, she is a patient of mine and I know the road to her is not yet open; and so grit your teeth, maintain your façade, and convey indifference!

And the others? I am alone again!

Edi Bibring: Always was and always will be a hypocritical philistine. But I like him—despite his vanity and pigheadedness!

Otto Fenichel: Still wearing his armor.

Lisl Brauner: I am very fond of her, although she is so difficult.

Berta Bornstein: An unimportant, pleasant plaything for leisure hours and hiking; a stupid, malicious feline, very homosexual, grasps people intuitively and very accurately.

Lia Laszky: Whom I must admire for the changes she has gone through in one year.

Hans Swarowski: Smart, amusing, superficial.

June 4

I intend to turn over a new leaf and be a more serious person. Yesterday I finished *The Lie**; it excited me greatly, although I had to laugh at myself—but I was not yet entirely able to do so! The last act, which had been written for so long, fit in with the others with no difficulty: he dies in the lie.

The symbol—as fulfillment of a wish!

The end!

June 12

Annie was given June 23 as a final date. If she were decent, *she* would have to resolve *my* transference *to her*.

June 14

Annie Pink!

I am writing because I would like to spare both you and myself the experience of a perhaps unpleasant moment which we might never have had to anticipate had I met you under different circumstances. Nor would I even have drafted this letter three months ago, but I hope and believe that you are now sufficiently advanced to read it with equanimity.

What I have to say is that I would like to give you all the love you deserve and that you are the second woman who I think could mean a great deal to me, change me, and make me happy. I have restrained myself for five months (God knows it was not easy!) because I first wanted to see you in good health and on your feet again before having to give me any consideration. And come what will, I shall always be happy if this has become a reality. After you have read this letter, do not come to me for analysis anymore. Come when you are ready to answer it, whatever the answer may be.

My decision has been reached—I have had six months in which to make it. Take your time in reaching yours, for you

*A play by Reich. [Eds.]

would need a lot of patience with me, I am a person who has emerged from the blackest depths and brought many an ugly trait along.

Live and be happy—I will wait.

Whatever the outcome, you may always count on me as a friend!

A dream: I am visiting the Brauners or have gone visiting somewhere with them. In a room, Lisl is sleeping, and I am with her. In another room to the left, there is a man sleeping, apparently Lisl's father. I see that the door is ajar. He passes through our room and finds me with Lisl. I put an end to the embarrassing situation by declaring that I want to marry Lisl, but in the same instant I remember that this will cause me to lose Annie, whom I love more. Lisl is happy—this amazes me. She is somehow changed, I share her happiness . . . I have forgotten the rest.

Residue from the day before the dream: a conversation with Lisl during which she remarked that it is a disgrace when a twenty-five-year-old man is not yet married. My written overture to Annie.

Recently I have been thinking about Annie more than I would like to. At one time I thought that my being her analyst would represent a great obstacle in her father's eyes. I love Annie and would not hesitate to marry her. I also feel that I could be very happy with her if she showed the necessary understanding of me and my faults. I am so fatigued and need a woman who loves me and whom I, too, can love fully. I really do believe that I am very capable of love (Lia once spoke of erotic power), and that capacity would be kindled if only I had a love object who was willing to receive. How about Annie? Again, I fear neurotic idiosyncrasies, on my side as well. The simplest way would be to send her the letter I have drafted. What can be said against it? The fact that I am her analyst? But even that would make little difference if Annie were really able to do what I suggest; namely, allow herself time for unbiased reflection. Also, she feels that she has stopped chasing after ideals. She has an urban and I a rustic personality. Can such individuals ever find each other? But of course they can; I even think that they would complement each other beautifully. My farmer's personality might well function as a strong support for her.

The other alternative: complete the analysis, resolve the transference (which, incidentally, does not seem to be particularly strong at the moment: Annie, it would be worth a try!), approach her later, let it evolve. But I fear the absence of transference (and to take advantage of it would be very mean!).

Furthermore, what speaks against the letter is the somewhat bourgeois, melodramatic nature of such a declaration, and then the inevitable tension and inhibition which would arise in both of us the next time we saw each other.

I shall wait.

Annie ought to study pedagogy and psychoanalysis. Then there would also be room for biology *and* lovely, practical activity!

I love Annie! It is entirely different from what it was before!

June 22

I have a feeling that after a three-year interlude I am returning to maturity and adulthood. It is different after the pubertal storms which took place between the ages of twenty-one and twenty-five, different, and somehow I am looking, searching for *the woman*, the essence of my emotional, physical, and intellectual being. *I need a woman, my woman*—how many times have I written that before! My wife, my girl, my mother, my woman! Is it an ideal I have set unattainably high? No, they do exist! They live and exist, the women who can accept a man as a child without his having to fear he must renounce his masculinity because of it. Male and female protoplasm—not a billy-goat stud and a goat-keeper.

Man and woman, not as each other's overseer but as understanding individuals with flexible, pliable contours.

Must I wait, in asceticism, because it has not yet come about?

No! Take, drink in the moment, and fill in the gaps, which, however, must not take on greater importance than what is actually present in reality. Youth is unhappy when it chases after ideals, happy when it can fill in the gaps, supply what is lacking without false emotions and distortion. I recognize my maturity, my longing for a female companion in the fact that I am beginning to feel the distortion when I attempt to fill in the gaps. It is a frequent thought but only rarely a *true emotion*: if only I had her, I would never look at another woman. Once I felt it —with Lia—when she was still a girl, half child, and had not yet landed in the Café Central. But, nevertheless, it was the whore who teased me. And Lore, that soul embodied in a woman, like Mother, tap, tap, here I am! Yes, there she was, yes, body and soul—but only her soul was permitted to express itself, her body lacked Annie's litheness, Lia's suppleness. Annie lacks the spiritual, "Tap, tap, here I am," a presence which takes you with a firm but motherly touch. Lore's soul, Annie's body and litheness, Lore's spiritual body, Annie's physical soul, to the extent that the psyche is an expression of the body and vice versa! Lore and Annie, both analyzed by me—and how different from each other, how typical and yet paradoxical their attitudes! Lore, the mother, came and said, "Here I am, take me and I will love you!" Annie, whose body makes her a whore, who will not come to me for fear of humiliating herself and has no idea how greatly she would elevate herself with a candid "I love you, take me!" She is incapable of love! Perhaps she will not say it to *me—but then she is incapable of saying it to anyone else, either; she would never forthrightly speak such words, as Lore would, even if she thought she felt love. Oh, what whorish pride*!

Cannot Lore's motherliness and spirituality be combined with Annie's body? Body and soul express themselves through each other and in me the body has the upper hand—think of Lore, Lia! The body will always drive me to ecstasy, restlessness, neurosis; while the soul will impel me toward peacefulness and motherliness—and I shall follow the body! For Lore's soul can never compensate for her body, since in me the physical impulses are dominant—although not secure enough to forgo spirituality entirely!

That is why I love Strindberg. He saw and experienced it as no other: being compelled to stay together with all the "You should do it this way," "No, that way," "Do this, if you please," "Do it that way"—which kills everything!

I know for sure: if an Annie–Lore does not appear, I shall always forsake Lore to go to Annie, spend myself on Annie and recover with Lore—and still love both.

They are the symbols of my sexuality!

And now to the question: to what extent can analysis unearth the original, female element, monogamy and maternal emotions, not to mention the actual reality of motherhood, when it has been pushed aside by its opposite, the element of lithe physicality (penis pride)? For this is the reason why whores do not want children—and here again we see a case of the body being victorious over the original elements. The body knows—for look at the woman who has borne four children! This, too, is a trap set by sexuality!

Is the following to be understood as an impulse toward a solution? The day before yesterday, Annie dreamed, for the first time in her life, of a child with whom she was playing. Is this to be her path—how will her body and the child get along together?

June 28

Annie has withdrawn from analysis! It was like the relief after a nightmare—only now do I realize how great a burden I had to bear over these last months!

I am pleased and hope that Annie will come to me—I love her . . .

June 30

Annie—Annie—is this a neurosis? I ask over and over. For, if it is, Annie shall never hear of it.

But no, it cannot be neurosis, for that would include her finding out and rejecting me. Perhaps it is a last remnant of doubt about meaning a great deal to someone? And yet . . .

I dream about Annie a lot, but the dreams are now of a different kind—more realistic, not exaggerated; only yesterday, it was in a meadow near Mödling, where I had once thought a great deal about her. Never before have I had the feeling beyond all doubt that marriage is forthcoming, never has a picture of togetherness entered my mind so forcibly as this time. I am not *in love* with Annie; *I love her, just as she is*, do not want to make her into anything, have no plans other than finding great happiness with this person. We are both the lonely, unsociable type (in contrast to Bernfeld and his circle), characteristics which result in anarchy, individualism. We do not wish to lead or to be led (Annie perhaps somewhat less than I), but are aware that possibilities lie only within the earthy, spiritual rewards of the family (how difficult the use of some words becomes, due to distortion!) and within love, a free-flowing, undemanding, natural love—which is the only path leading out of the Strindberg problem.

Bernfeld and his group, who find fulfillment when they are accepted into a gregarious herd (not a value judgment!)—are they the solution? Could a society composed of Bernfelds endure? They are incompatible with the concept of earthy, intellectual individuality! They have leaders and those who follow completely; polygamy and polyandry; outstanding minds who create from nothing. Bernfeld wants to have only two analyses and live from writing books. *I am gaining ever deeper insight into the fact that the more one progresses in understanding, the less courage one finds to write!*

It is not simple—and even if one sees many an issue more clearly in the quiet of the night, it is difficult to communicate one's thoughts to the world! Propaganda is useless. Individual "becoming" flows of itself from the source of one's own predisposition.

I am reading *Buddha*—it is an experience!*

*Georg Grimm, *Die Lehre des Buddha*. [Eds.]

Dear Annie Pink!

Your letter did not actually astonish me, but it did disquiet me despite the fact that I had been expecting it. When I heard of your illness, concern for you was the first thing to come to mind. But the intensity of your reaction to the discontinuance of analysis is exactly what shows me that you have been cured. On Tuesday you asked how the transference could be dissolved and I replied that there were two possibilities: to discuss it until the patient gets fed up or to break off, in which case a residue remains for a varying length of time. This is the way it will be with you: you are capable of freeing yourself from me if you just let the matter rest for a while. Thus, the last logical step would have been not to answer your letter.

I should have preferred to tell you this in person. Until now, I have spoken to you as a physician; as a human being, I have long had to wait in the background and hide behind my professional façade. Please try, Annie Pink, to see all that has happened and everything which I want to tell you now in a clear light.

You were under treatment with me for six and a half months. I came to know your neurosis and its etiology. But I also became acquainted with you, I saw you within the context of your neurosis: distorted, false, unnatural, and incapable of joy in life and of accomplishment. For unconscious reasons which you have come to know well enough, you were inclined toward an intellectual evaluation of people and things which gave you great unconscious pleasure while consciously it could only bring dissatisfaction. I saw the person who could become capable of joy and what it was that kept this from actually happening—and I rejoiced over that person; I rejoiced at the thought of creating the possibility of really seeing that person before me. Your health improved steadily; only occasionally was there distortion, stemming from the recent denial which you had to experience in order to gain complete health. And the joy I took in you grew from week to week; I had long exceeded the bounds of interest which a male physician is allowed to take in a female patient if he himself is to remain free of conflicts and capable of further work. It was not easy for me these last few months, Annie Pink. But I wanted, yes, I first had to make sure that you were healthy. And just as you struggled with the transference, I struggled with "countertransference"—I was surprised that you hadn't noticed.

But where does transference overlap with countertransference? The fact that you were my fourth female patient and I had never had any similar struggles told me more . . .

[No date]

Annie is going to make me ill again, for if she cannot or will not, then all coercion would be useless; and if she complied in spite of this, we would not find happiness.

In an all-night café   *3 a.m.*   *Sept. 18/19, 1921*

My dear, good Annie-child! Your ambivalence stems from your delicate instinct, for you sense something else in me, something which at present, and when I am with you, remains dormant. The dark, criminal, lethal elements within me! But they do exist—I feel it as I sit here—in this "dive," where a consumptive, syphilitic "musician" is seated at a grand piano, sadly, spinelessly playing merry yodeling songs to drunken men and whores. In another corner, staring eyes are looking to their cards for money. And I feel no disgust or repulsion at these poor people; four thin legs just danced a poor imitation of the spirited creation we usually call the waltz—music, the dance, Anniechen, there are two sides to everything! Today I casually remarked that I would go to seed in a dive or on the midden—I didn't believe it myself, it was just the usual kind of idle talk; nor do I believe it when I think that the intense hopes I place in you could gradually or suddenly diminish just because you also know the other side of me—which is in motion at this very moment, as a hellish racket erupts from syphilitic throats, and lusting skeletons with emaciated muscles embrace each other.

Perhaps matters are all right the way they stand—the events of the last few days have caused me once again to review my own personality, and I love you with all my potentialities, my filthy and my holy self. I love you so much that I suddenly feel myself sinking—to where I am now, a man torn between the spirit and the mire!

Would you have the strength to sit here and see the criminal in me, to experience it with your own eyes? Or shall you never see or hear it, for I love your tenderness and your weaknesses.

Oct. 5

I am now determined not to give up Annie's body and to take a firm stand: *Annie, I will not do without you!* Let us see: one of the following will come true:

1. She will run away from me.
2. She will run away from me and then return.
3. She will stay with me.

*   *   *

MY EARLY FORCED MARRIAGE

I met Annie Pink, whom I later married, for the first time at the symposium at Otto Fenichel's in June 1920. She was the daughter of a Viennese tradesman. She was a member of the Youth Movement and was studying for her high-school diploma. She was very reserved and secretly arrogant; she was not happy. She lived ascetically, suffered from compulsions, and wanted to be treated by me. She did not come to me when Lore was alive; when Lore, her friend, died, she came. The treatment lasted six months and helped her a little. She had the usual father-transference and I fell seriously in love with her. I mastered my attraction until the end of the therapy, but afterwards we saw each other regularly and became good friends. One lovely summer evening, we went for a walk in Grinzing. My arm rested in hers. There we encountered her stepmother, who was very friendly and smiled knowingly. The next day, Annie told me the old woman had congratulated her on her "engagement." She had answered that she had no intention of becoming engaged; this made her a "modern sexual rebel."

On a wonderful sunny Sunday, we went into the Wiener Wald. She desired me and I her. We had a deep feeling of belonging together. I corresponded somewhat to her hero fantasy, and she looked a little like my mother. She had lost a bit of her hardness by being so much in love; the mature woman had come to the fore. We were both young, intelligent, and strong. She had never embraced a man. We drove to the Sophienalpe. After we'd undressed, I embraced her. But she suddenly became cold and asked me to stop. I did so out of love for her, but I was utterly miserable. My body ached with excitement. We walked for some hours, taking the long way home. I decided silently not to continue the relationship and fell into my well-known depression. I accompanied her home. It was three o'clock in the morning, but still I went to a night club; I was in a lamentable mood. The next day, early in the morning, she came to me, entreating and loving. This time she accepted me, and we were very happy. I really loved her. She visited me often in my room, but she had to leave at night because of my landlady. We decided that from now on I should visit her at her home. She gave me a key to the house and to the door of her room, which had its own entrance off the main hall. When I visited her in the evenings with her parents, I left late and went to a nearby café and waited until I thought her parents were asleep. Then I crept silently to her like a criminal and she awaited me like a criminal as well. The forbidden did not in any way increase the pleasure, as clever people claim; we were afraid of being discovered. So it went for weeks. One night, I lay with her and we heard a noise as if someone were standing outside the door. Then the door opened quietly, very quietly, and a head appeared through the crack, looked for a long time, and went away. It was Malva, her stepmother. We were worried, but at the same time it amused us.

Early next morning, I was studying in my café. Her father, a very decent and liberal-minded man, came in. He was a Social

Democrat, member of the district administration, counsel to the poor, and a freethinker. He looked distressed. Curtly and with some embarrassment, he said that he knew everything and now we "had to get married." But we were not thinking of getting married. It is true that some weeks previously I had asked Annie to become my wife, but she had said that could wait. Now her father demanded it. He left and Annie came. She was angry, just as I was. We did not want to be forced into anything. We had taken a four-week tour that summer alone together, with the permission of her father, and naturally had enjoyed ourselves. Her parents had really not dreamed that Annie would commit the "indecency" of sleeping with me! Only an old aunt from Berlin had made nasty inquiries when we met her in Otztal. Now, as they demanded marriage, I gave in: I did want to live with her. Still, we were defiant, and the Sunday marriage we announced was a sham: there were no marriages at the registrar's office on Sundays. The reason we did this was simple: my brother was in Vienna with his girlfriend—his future wife—and was staying with me. Consequently Annie and I could no longer meet there. We therefore said that we were already married, and thus were allowed to sleep together in her room "entirely legally." Law and custom wanted it this way. So, on that questionable Sunday on which there had not been any kind of legalization of our embraces, there was a small celebration at six in the evening. Everyone knew the truth except her parents. The witnesses were our friends, and two other young people were also present. This was on March 12. On March 17 we were really married. But there was no celebration this time. Malva, the lascivious old thing, discovered, to our regret, that the marriage license was dated the 17th, and not the 12th of March 1922. There was a scene. We did not want to admit to the deception. We had rebelled against the forced marriage but had nevertheless obeyed. And the whole conflict arose from the fact that we could not and did not want to spend five days apart. But in spite of everything, we were very happy. We moved into a small apartment.

In the summer of 1922, I graduated as a doctor of medicine

from the University of Vienna. I had already been analyzing patients for more than three years, was a member of the Psychoanalytic Society, and was involved in various clinical investigations.

To the horror of my friends, who were dressed in morning coat or tuxedo, I hurried to my graduation ceremony from an analytic session, dressed in a light summer suit. It was noticeable, but not too bad. Formal attire was not obligatory, and besides, I did not have any. I do not like ceremonial occasions. There was no one there who would have congratulated me, as did the many relatives of hopeful academics. I knew that for me the diploma alone did not make much of a practical difference. Only my mother's good wishes would have made me happy.